For our readers and members.

Introduction

"We don't have an endless amount of time," is how Sen. Bernie Sanders (I-Vt.) announced his presidential candidacy. Sort of. The democratic socialist made the remark at the top of a press conference in April 2015, when he revealed he would be running for the White House. The utterance was neither a reference to the warming of the planet nor the shrinking of Americans' real incomes. Nor was it meant to allude to Corporate America's grip on the US government and the impending calamities they portend. Sanders was on his lunch break and on the grounds of the US Capitol—limiting what he could say and do, per federal finance laws and his daily workload. "I've got to get back," he said.

Although it was a throw-away remark, we latched onto it. Not only was Sanders foreshadowing his Larry David sending-up, with an introduction to his observational style, it casually evinced a scrappiness and an awareness he has demonstrated time and time since: "Let's get on with this."

While far from perfect, Sanders has proven that Americans can credibly challenge their millionaire and billionaire overlords. Americans who have suffered for decades under a neoliberal consensus don't want to wait any longer for someone to tear it down. They don't have an endless amount of time, either.

It is something we identify with. When we started *The District Sentinel*, we set out to create a progressive record to help document how callous elites and poisonous conventional wisdom dominate Washington—and how they can both be challenged. Like Sen. Sanders, we set out to do it on something of a wing and prayer. We hope to one day have a small sliver of the impact that he has already made.

To that end, we published *We Don't Have an Endless Amount of Time: A First Draft of 2015*. It documents our first full year of progressive policy and legislative journalism in Washington DC, covering a rage of topics. Issues discussed include: the Iran Deal, criminal justice reform, the Mediterranean Refugee Crisis, corporate dominance of trade policy and Wall Street, and, of course, Sen. Sanders' campaign.

The book focuses on stories we covered throughout the year, with some personal anecdotes intertwined, and fills in the gaps by highlighting important reports written by others. *We Don't Have An Endless Amount of Time* paints a picture about the activities of the United States government throughout 2015, and helps explain why the presidential campaign—at least on the Democratic side—has thus far been characterized by informed mistrust of the status quo.

TABLE OF CONTENTS

1. *Letters to a Decapitator*

When we launched *The District Sentinel*, we expected to use the word "ridiculous" in our coverage of US foreign policy, but not straight away, and not while quoting a State Department spokesperson. That is, however, as luck would have it, what transpired on our first week of publication.

During a press conference like many others, Jen Psaki, then department spokesperson, was fending off inquiries by trying to say as much as possible without actually communicating anything of substance. The topic that tripped her up: an Egyptian judge's acquittal of the country's former dictator, Hosni Mubarak. The ousted president and former US ally had been charged with murdering 239 of the 900 protesters killed by his security forces in 2011, during the popular uprising that preceded his immediate resignation. But in late 2014, he was found not guilty under a government that had itself, the year before, overthrown his successor: Egypt's only democratically-elected president, Mohammed Morsi. As Mubarak's regime had, the military government, led by Gen. Adbel Fatah el-Sisi, enjoyed strong support from Washington. It suddenly became difficult for the State Department to explain.

"Generally, we continue to believe that upholding impartial standards of accountability will advance the political consensus on which Egypt's long-term stability and economic growth depends," Psaki said, of the Mubarak ruling. "But beyond that I would refer you to the Egyptian government for any further comment."

The diplomatic press corps was unimpressed. "What you said says nothing," AP veteran Matt Lee shot back during the ensuing melee. "It's like saying 'we support the right of people to breathe.' That's great, but if you can't breathe," he added, before Psaki cut him off, refusing to elaborate.

After the briefing ended, as the TV lights dimmed, Lee approached the podium and Psaki immediately volunteered an explanation. "That Egypt line is ridiculous," she sighed. Lee chortled.[1]

It was a rare peek behind the curtain, caught for all to see on the State Department's livefeed—a reminder that not even American officials believe all of their highfalutin horseshit. It was also quite the moment for us. We were doing practice coverage during the briefing and pushed our debut up a few days when we realized no one else caught it on the record. After publication, the story was picked up by a number of outlets, from *BuzzFeed* to DemocracyNow! to Fox News. Psaki apologized for her hot mic moment when asked about it by ABC News (although the State Department declined to respond to *The Sentinel's* initial request for comment).

And then Washington moved on (Psaki herself moved on to become White House Communications Director in April 2015). "Ridiculous" foreign policy is the rule, not an exception, inside the Beltway.

In **JANUARY**, for example, when King Abdullah of Saudi Arabia died at the tender age of 90, President Obama hailed him as "dedicated to the education of his people and to greater engagement with the world." And the Pentagon decided to mark the passing of Abdullah by reaching into its freedom-spreading arsenal and grabbing its pens: it held an essay contest to honor the late monarch. "This is an important opportunity to honor the memory of the king, while also fostering scholarly research on the Arab-Muslim world," said Joint Chief of Staffs Chair Gen. Martin Dempsey. [2]

In October, however, when asked to comment on how the Saudi Monarchy routinely[i] enforces that dedication by the mother of Ali Mohammed Baqir al-Nimr—a dissident teen sentenced to death by Riyadh, by public crucifixion and decapitation—President Obama was silent. When pressed about the case by reporters in September, State Department spokesperson Mark Toner said: "We've talked about our concerns about some of the capital punishment cases in Saudi Arabia in our Human Rights Report, but I don't have any more to add to it." Nor

---

[i]   According to the State Department's 2013 Human Rights Report, Saudi Arabia is characterized by

did his bosses, the leader of the Free World and his chief envoy.

Toner did, however, note that day, in response to a question about another development in the news, that the US "would welcome" Saudi Arabia's chairing of the UN Human Rights Council.[3] He made these remarks deliberately and into a microphone that he knew was recording his statements.

* * *

One could be forgiven for believing that these obscene pro-Saudi policies would cause the president's most strident opponents on the Right to lash out at him, despite Riyadh's geopolitical importance. Congress, after all, is rife with both Islamophobia and urges to incessantly crow about American superiority—particularly within the Republican caucus (see Chapter 11 for more on the former).

But the Right furiously blasted the administration for not being sufficiently deferential to the Saudi Monarchy—even as it was gearing up to embark on one of the year's most brutal campaigns: the invasion of Yemen, which it led in the Spring.

"Isn't that quite a commentary on our relationship with Saudi Arabia and the other thirteen countries in their coalition—that they would, literally, the day of their attacks, tell the United States of America that they're going to launch a major campaign?" Senate Armed Services Committee chair John McCain (R-Ariz.) raged at Gen. Lloyd Austin, commander of CENTCOM[ii], in March. "I mean, that is really a fantastic indicator of the deterioration of the trust and confidence that these countries, particularly Saudi Arabia, have in us," McCain added, saying the late notice proves correct "people [who] think it's better to be an enemy of the United States than a friend."[4]

[ii]   United States Central Command—the arm of the Pentagon that oversees operations in the Middle East, North Africa, and Central Asia.

But rather than dismissing the ravings or seeing the upside in a bit of daylight between Washington and a Wahhabi state, the administration took the basic substance of McCain's criticism to heart.

After a final outline to the Iran nuclear deal was finalized later in the Spring, President Obama organized a symposium to reassure our Sunni monarch allies of our undying love. [5] By October, the administration reported that the coming-together cultivated something of a more cordial friendship with the Saudis.

"I think relations with our Gulf allies have improved quite dramatically due to the work on the Camp David Summit and our security guarantees and trying to reassure them of our permanent commitment to their security," Assistant Secretary of State Anne Patterson told the Senate Foreign Relations Committee.[6]

In the same hearing, she explained how, simultaneously, the administration's Middle East policy agenda has shifted, and cited counterterrorism as "our first priority." "The second is human rights and democracy and economic growth," Patterson said. She described the administration as having "evolved" on these issues.

"I think there was perhaps an overly optimistic impression that we could focus on democracy promotion and economic growth in places like Egypt, and North Africa and even in the Levant," she added. "That has proven to be exceedingly difficult."

Not everyone on the inside had agreed, evidently, with the spirit of this evolution. Unnamed Obama administration officials told *Politico* about 36 hours earlier that they were regretting supporting the Saudi incursion into Yemen, with a specific fear of "abetting war crimes in a bombing campaign that could ultimately strengthen Islamist militants." The report noted Riyadh had been accused of killing 1,500 civilians.[7]

* * *

The initiative that, perhaps, most clearly illustrated Selective Washington Outrage last year actually sought to effectively correct decades of "ridiculous" policy.

In the final weeks of 2014, President Obama and Raul Castro shocked the world when they announced an imminent resumption of normal relations between Washington and Havana—the first since 1961. "Neither the American, nor Cuban people are well served by a rigid policy that is rooted in events that took place before most of us were born," President Obama said.[8]

Cold Warriors came out of the woodwork and had Three Mile Island-scale meltdowns. Reliably militaristic Democrats like Rep. Eliot Engel (R-N.Y.) and Sen. Bob Menendez (D-N.J.) hit out at President Obama. The majority of huffing, as expected, came from the right, led by Sen. Marco Rubio (R-Fla.). "Tyrants around the world know that the US can be had," he bemoaned.[9]

Of course, they already knew this from Rubio's own press releases. The senator had, the previous month, held a meeting and a photo-op with Honduras' authoritarian president Juan Orlando Hernandez. Rubio said US support for the repressive Central American police state "is key to addressing some of the most pressing security threats of our hemisphere."[10]

The NGO community would disagree. Human Rights Watch noted that Honduran "journalists and peasant activists are particularly vulnerable to violence" amid "chronic" abuses of power by cops. [11]

"Honduras suffers from rampant crime and impunity for human rights abuses," HRW said. "The murder rate was again the highest in the world in 2014."

Not that the Honduran government nor the United States enabling of it was a major issue in 2015. Washington largely didn't care about its abuses, since it seized power in a 2009 coup—one legitimized by the Obama

13

administration in the face of a hemispheric outcry.[12] At least some House members took exception in August and demanded that the US stop backing Central American death squads like Reagan was still in charge.

Reps. Raul Grijalva (D-Ariz.) and Keith Ellison (D-Minn.)[iii] and nineteen of their colleagues wrote to John Kerry, calling on the administration to freeze security assistance "until human rights abuses are adequately addressed by the Honduran government." No Republicans signed on.

Fortunately, for supporters of the unfolding Cuba detente itself—which is to say, the majority of the country and a supermajority of the world—the saboteurs don't seem capable of making coexistence unprofitable. Moderate Republicans, such as Sens. Jeff Flake (R-Ariz.) and Mike Enzi (R-Wyo.), threw their weight behind the administration, declaring that isolation hadn't led to Cuba embracing capitalism; it had just led to lost opportunities for Corporate America.

"Some will say that we ought to receive something in exchange for this, that if we're giving up something, we ought to get some concession from the Cuban government," Flake said in support of a bill that would relax sanctions. "I think we all need to remember this is a sanction, or prohibition on Americans, not Cubans."[13]

Across the aisle, there was nothing but enthusiastic agreement with this sentiment. Sen. Debbie Stabenow (D-Mich.) remarked that now is the time "to provide greater access to the Cuban people to American products and more democratic ideas."

We're definitely good at the product access bit. And by the end of the summer, the Obama administration had swapped envoys with Havana and had loosened commercial and travel restrictions.

But Congress still won't lift the embargo. Maybe another fifty years of

---

[iii]   The Congressional Progressive Caucus co-chairs.

economic deprivation caused by right-wing Americans will show them that capitalism is actually good.

2. *Fission Accomplished*

Respectable critics of President Obama's foreign policy wanted you to know in 2015 that they were appalled by the suggestion they want an Iraq-style invasion of Iran. "The President is wonderful at setting up straw men," John McCain crowed in the spring on the Hugh Hewitt Show. "He's saying we have a choice between this and all-out war. Not true, sir. Excuse me, Mr. President, not true. We could increase the sanctions."[14]

The truth however, is that we could not. The participation of other permanent UN Security Council members—Russia, China, the UK and France—were what gave the penalties real bite, and they had only agreed to implement them on the understanding that Washington was interested in signing a deal. John "Bomb Bomb-Bomb, Bomb-Bomb Iran" wasn't exactly being forthright in that right-wing talk radio interview.

But it didn't take the basic understanding of multilateral diplomacy that McCain evidently lacks to see that some in Congress were pining for the days of 2002-2003. It was splashed all over the press releases and their red faces. The way hawkish lawmakers conducted themselves evoked memories of George W. Bush mangling his way through David Frum's war erotica.

In **FEBRUARY**, for example, a group with close ties to the Mujahhedin-e-Khalq (MEK)[iv] produced a report alleging that Tehran was maintaining a "secret nuclear facility" called Lavizan-3.[15] The dossier, published by the National Council of Resistance of Iran (NCRI), was picked up on Feb. 23 by *The Washington Post*, not long after the story first spewed forth from the bowels of *The Washington Free Beacon;* a comically unreliable lobbyist-founded online yellow rag.

[iv] A Paris-based Iranian pro-regime change organization that has been widely described as a personality cult. It was considered a Foreign Terrorist Organization by the State Department until 2012, after a lengthy, well-financed lobbying campaign that employed many former high-ranking American political figures like Howard Dean and Newt Gingrich.

The investigation's merits were, unsurprisingly, subsequently and rapidly torn asunder by some rando online. A Daily Kos blogger noted the NCRI "evidence" included a photograph that, per a simple reverse image search, appeared lifted from an Iranian safe company's website.[16] Nonetheless, on Feb. 24, a pair of Congressmen pressed John Kerry on the contents of the report.

Rep. Dana Rohrabacher (R-Calif.) told him that "our friends in the MEK" had tipped us off, and asked if "the Mullah regime" informed US negotiators "about the existence of this nuclear facility." Rep. Brad Sherman (D-Calif.) meanwhile, said that "the MEK sometimes gives us accurate information" and wanted to know about IAEA inspections of Lavizan-3.

Kerry said the administration takes such accusations into careful consideration, and that these were still under review. Three days later, however, the State Department told *The Sentinel*—in diplomatic terms, of course—that the NCRI's conclusion was baloney.

"We have seen these claims and while we take all such reports seriously, we do not believe that this allegation has merit or that it impacts our ongoing negotiations over Iran's nuclear program," an official said in an emailed statement. "We have examined the report and have no information to support the conclusion reached by the group that made the allegations."[17]

Certain legislative aides and their bosses may have had a not-too-dissimilar analysis if they had fully employed Google image search capabilities.

* * *

A better and more prominent example of pre-Iraq-style garrulousness on Capitol Hill in 2015 was the open threat sent on March 9 to Iranian leaders. Love, Most of the Republican Senate Caucus.

Forty-seven GOP senators led by Sen. Tom Cotton (R-Ark.) told the Supreme Leader et. al that the deal was an executive agreement that a Republican president would nullify "with the stroke of a pen," and that Tehran neither understood this nor, generally speaking, how the United States government worked.

"We hope this letter enriches your knowledge of our constitutional system and promotes mutual understanding and clarity as nuclear negotiations progress," they concluded.[18]

The guys who are secretively working to assemble a complex nuclear weapon also don't get "Schoolhouse Rocks," apparently.

Deliciously, the missive ended up raising questions about Republicans own enriched knowledge of "our constitutional system." Jack Goldsmith, assistant attorney general under George W. Bush, said that the Senate, actually, doesn't "ratify" treaties; and that while the distinction between ratification and the granting of "advice and consent" might be technical, "in a letter purporting to teach a constitutional lesson, the error is embarrassing."[19]

Moreover, there were murmurs about Cotton and his co-signers infringing upon more than the President's traditional prerogative. Members of the press queried whether the lawmakers violated an arcane 18th Century law called the Logan Act; a statute prohibiting American citizens from meddling in foreign "disputes or controversies" and working "to defeat the measures of the United States."

The possibility of 47 percent of the Senate being indicted on obscure charges might have been remote (and rightly so). It, nonetheless, added to the amateurishness of the initiative, and the State Department seemed to revel in the wind-twisting.

"I'm not aware of any conversations within the United States government regarding whether Sen. Cotton and the other signatories violated the Logan Act," spokesperson Jen Psaki told reporters. But she wouldn't explicitly rule out the possibility. "This is a legal act and I'd certainly defer to others on that," Psaki added.[20]

The Iranians, to their credit, weren't shaken. The Foreign Ministry replied that Cotton et al. "not only do not understand international law, but are not fully cognizant of the nuances of their own Constitution when it comes to presidential powers in the conduct of foreign policy."

Foreign Minister Javad Zarif personally added that the senators "may not fully understand that in international law, governments represent the entirety of their respective states, are responsible for the conduct of foreign affairs, are required to fulfill the obligations they undertake with other states and may not invoke their internal law as justification for failure to perform their international obligations."[21]

It might be hard to get completely owned by a man who represents a theocratic government, but Senate Republicans found a way.

Although his attempts to "enrich" Iranians' while stopping their uranium enrichment failed spectacularly, Cotton himself walked away no poorer (politically speaking) for his efforts. He appeared later in March as an emerging right-wing leader at an "off the record" event hosted by the National Defense Industrial Association; a trade group run by executives from America's top weapons manufacturers (per *The Intercept's* Lee Fang: "Northrop Grumman, L-3 Communications, Mantech International, Boeing, Oshkosh Defense and Booz Allen Hamilton, among other firms").

In April, Cotton did right by his hosts and called for a $1 trillion annual Pentagon budget—an increase of about $388 billion. "Our experiment with retreat must end," he said.[22]

* * *

So bountiful were the GOP's shameless attacks on the Iran Deal that Cotton's March letter wasn't even, at the time, the most hotly contested sabre-rattling maneuver that year. In January, the day after the President's State of the Union, Speaker of the House John Boehner (R-Ohio) invited Benjamin Netanyahu to address Congress—to trash the initiative and President Obama's policy, as he had done throughout negotiations. The Israeli PM accepted the offer.

No self-respecting adult should have expected Netanyahu to act with restraint in the face of White House opposition to the invitation. "Bibi" and many of his Israeli counterparts have, since the early nineties, warned of an imminent Iranian nuclear threat, and the Israeli leader seemed to relish publicly shrieking about it whenever he could—particularly during his current premiership, as Gaza has become increasingly uninhabitable and the West Bank host to more and more Israeli settlements. Yet in spite of the slow-motion build-up to Netanyahu's oratory trainwreck, at least one key Dem was dismayed by what she heard.[v]

"[A]s one who values the US–Israel relationship, and loves Israel, I was near tears throughout the Prime Minister's speech," Nancy Pelosi (D-Calif.) said, ripping Bibi's claim that the deal "paves Iran's path to the bomb." The House Minority Leader accused Netanyahu of having delivered a public "insult to the intelligence of the United States"[23] She simply expected more from a guy who has indiscriminately shelled schools and refugee camps and considers children of his own Arab citizens to be a "demographic problem."[24]

Of course, Democrats wouldn't stay mad at Bibi for too long, as the House Minority Leader alluded to in the preface of her denunciation. After the speech and after Netanyahu's March reelection, the White House said it would "reevaluate" its position on vetoing 1 Palestinian statehood resolutions at the UN Security Council, in light of Netanyahu's far-right election campaign. But the administration had no intention of doing any

---

[v]   One Republican, also skipped out. Rep. Walter Jones (R-NC)—uncharacteristically skeptical of the US-Israel relationship for a United States Congressman, let alone a Republican one—Insisted, however, it wasn't a "protest," declaring he never attends joint addresses "to listen to the foreign leaders." https://www.districtsentinel.com/republican-lawmaker-hated-by-israel-lobby-wont-attend-netanyahu-speech-but-its-not-to-protest/

such thing.[25] A *Politico* report published months later said the White House was "opposed to the Palestinians going the UN route, but...Obama wouldn't make a public declaration himself."[26]

And in May, the administration confirmed that it had joined Israel in opposition to a multilateral agreement on, of all things, an initiative toward a nuclear weapons-free Middle East. State Department Spokesperson Jeff Rathke said that the proposal was "unbalanced" and "on terms that would not allow for consensus-based discussions among all regional states." When pressed by *Al-Quds* reporter Said Arikat to describe what a "balanced" draft might look like, however, Rathke would not elaborate.[27] Tel Aviv's undeclared nuclear program loomed large over the discussion.

And when the European Union had the audacity to make its member states more aware of the Israeli Occupation—by labeling goods produced in the internationally-recognized occupied territories as coming from there—Senate Dems didn't shy from siding with Republicans and Standing With Israel, as they have done for years, in its ongoing struggle to wipe Palestine off the map.

"Differentiating between products made by Israeli companies creates a troubling precedent that could eventually lead to the type of activities that [trade promotion] provisions aim to address," they wrote in a petition organized by Sens. Ted Cruz (R-Texas) and Kirsten Gillibrand (D-N.Y.). The letter cited legislation passed earlier in the year calling on US trade negotiators to fight boycotts of Israel. Neither the words "occupation" nor "settlement" were used. Ten Democratic Senators signed the letter, including prominent reformers Cory Booker (D-N.J.) and Ron Wyden (D-Ore.) [28]

* * *

Amid the fretting over Iran's nuclear capable Sword of Damocles that failed to hang over Israel for a quarter-century, there was some discussion of what US-Iran relations themselves might look like, as the deal began to take effect.

21

In October, that discussion changed rather quickly when Iran's Supreme Leader Ali Khamenei, prohibited its reformist president Hassan Rouhani from pursuing any kind of deeper normalization with the US. The Ayatollah described the developing relationship as "[concentrated] on enmity toward the Establishment of the Islamic Iran [sic]" and "aimed at [paving the way for] infiltration."

"The enemies are trying to change [our] officials' calculations and influence the thoughts of people, particularly youths, and everyone should be vigilant and conscious [to prevent this]," Khamenei said.[29]

Throughout negotiations, the State Department was chilly to the idea of broader "rapprochement." In March, then-Deputy Spokesperson Marie Harf told reporters not to expect the deal to automatically trigger normalized ties, and got into a back-and-forth with reporters about the English definition of the word.[30] The completion of a final agreement, however, appeared to have changed institutional thinking—or at least what State was ready to admit publicly. In August, John Kerry relayed at a public forum in Manhattan how Rouhani's delegation "said to me: 'If we can get this deal done, then we're ready to sit down and talk about the regional issues.'"

"We owe it to the world to try to put it to the test," Kerry mused. "It would be diplomatic malpractice not to go out and try to explore that possibility, and we'll do so with our eyes wide open."[31]

But because of the Ayatollah's orders, it wasn't to be. It did, however, seem to legitimate President Obama's controversial statement—that the same right-wingers in Washington who accused him of "capitulating" to Iran shared an interest with their conservative counterparts in Tehran.

"Hardliners [in Iran] chanting 'Death to America' who have been most opposed to the deal...are making a common cause with the Republican Caucus," the president said, much to the right's horror.[32]

"I think the president has demeaned and cheapened the office of the presidency by that kind of comment," McCain groused.[33]

Better to use it to fight wars over phantom nuclear weapons.

3. #BreakTheInternet

The Obama administration set out in 2015 to do something that Kim Kardashian's bare ass couldn't, and that's #BreakTheInternet; or at least the confidence underpinning the sharing of sensitive information online.

"Tech execs say privacy should be the paramount virtue," FBI Director James Comey pleaded with lawmakers, in **MARCH**. "When I hear that, I close my eyes and say try to imagine what the world looks like where pedophiles can't be seen, kidnappers can't be seen, drug dealers can't be seen."

"I think it's going to require some sort of legislative fix." Comey was arguing for a cop-accessible backdoor to encrypted communications.[34]

The White House generally agreed, as did many other leaders of government agencies.

"None of these technology companies want to be in a position where they are aiding and abetting people who wants to use this technology to carry out an act of violence or carry out an act of terrorism," Josh Earnest had said in January.[35]

"If these are the paths that criminals, foreign actors, terrorists are going to use to communicate, how do we access that?" NSA Director Adm. Mike Rogers had asked in February. "We have shown in other areas that through both technology, a legal framework, and social compact that we have been able to take on tough issues. I think we can do the same thing here."[36]

Then, two months after Comey's March testimony, newly sworn-in Attorney General Loretta Lynch chimed in. "We are seeing many more people involved in terrorism investigations using peer-to-peer communications, specifically encrypted communications—communications that are designed to disappear once they are sent," she claimed. Lynch relayed to Congress that she had "grave concerns" about how cryptology hampers law enforcement.[37]

Everyone with significant authority in the administration was seemingly on the same page. There was, however, a problem. What Comey wanted was, technically, unfeasible. And more than that, it was a threat to securing *all* information online.

"It's impossible to build a backdoor just for the good guys," said Rep. Jason Chaffetz (R-Utah) in April. "If someone at the Genius Bar can figure it out, so can the bad guys in a van down by the river." He countered the administration's theory that large swaths of the internet were "going dark" (as Comey first put it, in October 2014) by pointing out what any teen trying to plan a house party on Facebook knows: we're living in a "golden age of surveillance for law enforcement."

Across the aisle, Rep. Ted Lieu (D-Calif.) said he "took offense" with the administration's testimony. "To me, it is very simple to draw a privacy balance when it comes to law enforcement," Lieu barked. "Just follow the damn constitution." He noted that "encryption only for good guys is technologically stupid." It's like trying to create a bullet that only kills bad guys.[38]

By July, the FBI Director changed his tune. In testimony before the Senate Judiciary Committee, Comey said that "there has not yet been a decision whether to seek legislation" mandating backdoor access to encrypted data.[39] And in September, *The Washington Post* reported that the administration had completely retreated from a legislative ask.[40]

Buried in the *Post's* story, however, was the documentation of an ODNI[vi] memo stressing the importance of "keeping our options open."

"The legislative environment is very hostile today," its author, General Counsel Robert Litt, wrote. But public sentiment "could turn in the event

---

[vi]   Office of the Director of National Intelligence

of a terrorist attack."

The prophecy nearly came true in November, after Islamic State militants carried out massacres in Paris. Within days of the attacks, government officials stateside were citing unverified reports claiming that the attackers used encrypted communications to organize their bloodshed. Lawmakers reacted as Litt had hoped.

"We're going to have legislation," John McCain (R-Ariz.) said four days after the attacks. He was joined by many others, including Senate Intelligence Committee leaders. Ranking Member Dianne Feinstein (D-Calif.) promised "some proposals that make some good sense."[41]

But a once-embarrassed James Comey couldn't match their enthusiasm. "Good people have made a decision to design products and sell products where court orders are ineffective," he said. "I'm not impugning their motives—I understand they see it as a competitive issue, or they think it's just the right thing to do."

Comey wouldn't, however, give up on the idea of using state muscle to, one day, pry open a corner of the internet where some semblance of privacy remains. "The question we have to ask ourselves," he said, "is there a way to get folks to change their business model so that judges orders can be complied with?"[42]

As our readers are probably aware, by publication, the FBI has attempted just that, by getting a magistrate judge to order Apple to hack into a mass shooter's iPhone.

* * *

In a separate campaign against online privacy in 2015, the President and Congress broadened the realm of digital information collected by the US government.

"One of the things in the new year that I hope congress is prepared to work with us on is stronger cybersecurity laws that allow for information sharing across private sector platforms, as well as the public sector," President Obama had said in late 2014.[43]

The president was seizing on enormous security breach suffered the prior month by Sony Entertainment. The resulting panic breathed life into a July 2014 initiative to grant unprecedented legal immunity to private corporations who pass on info related to "cyber threats" to the Feds. By April, The House and Senate were marking up legislation that would later take shape as the Cybersecurity Information Sharing Act (CISA).

"So-called 'insta-sharing' provisions in most of these bills would ensure that personal information feeds directly into the NSA's databases," Amie Stepanovich, US policy manager for Access, an online civil liberties advocate group told *The Sentinel*.[44] Under the law, Americans would be deprived of one remaining legal avenue of recourse against the surveillance state: the right to sue a tech company-turned-informant without the normal due process.

Opponents of CISA also noted that the bill's focus on intelligence-gathering failed to actually enhance cyber-threat prevention. Many attacks are conducted with relatively unsophisticated methods that prey on human error; such as the ubiquitous "phishing" attacks that fool users into giving up their passwords (what led to the Sony hack).

"If information-sharing legislation does not include adequate privacy protections, then that's not a cybersecurity bill—it's a surveillance bill by another name," longtime civil libertarian Ron Wyden said in March.

The opposition to CISA in the Senate was sufficient to derail a shady June attempt by Majority Leader Mitch McConnell (R-Ky.) to attach it to an amendment of the annual defense policy bill. Critics, including Leahy, noted that the Senate Intelligence Committee hadn't even marked-up the legislation with "a public hearing or public debate."[45]

Ultimately, the privacy camp was out-muscled. Although major tech companies like Apple, Google, and Twitter opposed CISA, major corporate lobbyists threw their weight for the first time behind it. CISA boosters reveled in the significance of the endorsement, when it was placed on the legislative agenda in October.

"This is the first time the Chamber of Commerce has come on a bill," Sen. Feinstein (D-Calif.) said, during a floor debate. "This is the first time we have virtually all the big employers of banks and other companies and retailers on a bill."

On Oct. 27, CISA passed the Senate in a 74-21 vote. To rub salt in the wounds, the body first rejected privacy safeguards. One would have narrowed the definition of a "cybersecurity threat." Another would have restricted what could be shared in real-time with the Department of Homeland Security—by tasking companies with scrubbing "PII" (personal identifiable information).[46]

"We've always been told this is about threats, this is about threats to our country, our institutions," Wyden told reporters, making his case for the latter amendment. "Why do you need people's personal information?"

President Obama's hope in 2015 to get "stronger cybersecurity laws" was thus fulfilled, enabling "network-speed" government omnipresence. In December, Congress put a classic DC cherry on top, jamming CISA into a year-end omnibus bill. The president signed it into law just before Christmas.

* * *

If the Obama administration deserves scorn from progressives for unrelentingly pushing internet surveillance, it deserves praise, on the other hand, for seeking to ensure that its biggest source of intelligence stays as relevant as possible.

In late February 2015, months after the President called for it to act, the

FCC[vii] approved sweeping new "Net Neutrality" rules, prohibiting internet service providers from discriminating against certain online content creators. After the Democrats' midterm drubbing, it was an unexpected but significant victory for freedom-of-expression advocates warning of a creeping pay-for-access web; the kind that might slowly lead to a cable television-style blanding of the internet.[47]

The FCC also moved to protect publicly-owned utilities that offer fast and cheap internet to communities underserved by oligopolistic telecoms giants; places like Chattanooga, Tenn and Wilson, N.C. that have established so-called municipal broadband. In February, the commission voted 3-2 along party lines to preempt laws in both states that prohibited the foundation and expansion of the locally-owned ISPs.

"Let us be clear," FCC Chair Tom Wheeler said, "this decision is pro-broadband, this decision is pro-competition, this decision is for the right of Americans through their elected local officials to make their own decision about their broadband future."

These fights are far from over. Along with legal challenges filed this year against the FCC, Republican majorities in both chambers of Congress have bills to disrupt the commission's ability to protect internet access.

But there's hope, for now, at least, that the potential breadth of internet enclosure has reached its outer limit. At a minimum, Americans can be assured that, until he leaves office, President Obama will fight for their right to access reams of information inconvenient to telecoms giants. But only as long as federal agents can get a peak over their shoulder.

[vii]   Federal Communications Commission

4. A Socialist Steps Up to Save America

Here at *The Sentinel*, we can't say the words "millionaires" or "billionaires" anymore without affecting a Brooklyn accent and imitating the hand flailing that has come to personify the Junior Senator from Vermont. And we have a feeling we're not alone.

You could argue that few politicians in 2015 made as significant of an impact as Bernie Sanders, who kicked it all off in **APRIL**, by telling reporters outside the Senate, on his lunch break, that he would be running for President.

He couldn't even directly make the case for his candidacy, per campaign finance laws, because he was on the grounds of the US Capitol.[48]

"We don't have an endless amount of time," Sanders fretted at the onset. "I have to get back." The self-proclaimed democratic socialist then enumerated the country's growing systemic economic problems, prescribing as a possible antidote, "any candidate who's not a billionaire, or who is not beholden to the billionaire class." It was a scenario he admitted doubting as possible. Sanders then went back to his day job.

It was all rather uncommon in the era of the focus-grouped, manicured-to-death presidential campaign. Indeed, if Sanders was intent on challenging the realm of possibility, he set the tone of his bid from the get-go, flaunting the grass-roots savvy that has seen him rise from Mayor of Burlington, Vt. to become the first socialist in US history to ever serve in what progressives used to call "the millionaires club."[viii]

Over the intervening months, Bernie's bid would dramatically transform from thought experiment to real pragmatic progressivism, enlisting millions of Americans in what has become a viable bid for the White

---

[viii] For a good reason—senators were not required to face direct election until the 17th Amendment was passed in 1913.

House.

$* * *$

But it was always clear from the beginning, that the devoutly-populist Sanders campaign would meet fierce resistance from the business-friendly Democratic Party elite, which viewed any primary challenge, let alone one from the left, as obstructing a formality—the nomination of former Secretary of State Hillary Clinton. In January, the *National Journal* reported that party officials envisioned "a scenario where Hillary is the only kind of serious credible candidate, in which case they might want zero debates or very, very few."[49]

And just hours after Sander's announcement, House Minority Leader Nancy Pelosi declined to say anything about the proposed coronation route, when asked if the party should hold formalized debates. "It's not up to me," she said. "If we don't have it, then we'll just get moving with what we have."[50]

Two weeks later, Senate Majority Leader Harry Reid (D-Nevada) also brushed off his colleague. "Right now we have Hillary Clinton. And that's it," he told MSNBC.[51]

Within months though, the party would learn it could not ignore the appeals from the Vermont senators' supporters; neither the democratic nor the socialistic ones. Come summer, Sanders would triple his support in national polls, from roughly 7 percent in April to over 21 percent by August. At the end of the summer, he started drawing crowds around the country in the five digits, mirroring the sort of rally-turnout that then-Sen. Barack Obama (D-Ill.) would get in 2008, when he was launching his once-improbable challenge of Clinton.

Reid might not have particularly wanted him, but the Senate Majority Leader had his rock star: a Doc Brown-looking-guy with an eighties folk album and a whole lot to say about marginal tax rates.

By July, the White House was forced to acknowledge that Bernie was tapping into a rich vein of discontent—though, without mentioning the senator's name. "It's clear that there's a lot of energy on the Democratic side of the aisle and I think that is a good thing," Josh Earnest carefully told reporters. "Seeing a lot of democratic leaning voters charged up and excited about politics and participating in a political event is something that we're pleased to see."[52]

In other ways, the White House was definitely not Feeling the Bern. Sanders, after all, had been among those in the Dem caucus who stuck their necks out to oppose President Obama's push to form another free-trade agreement: the Trans-Pacific Partnership (see Chapter Six). Though Clinton dutifully lobbied for the sweeping deal as Obama's Secretary of State—calling it, at one point, the "gold standard" of trade agreements— she reversed tack in the autumn. With Sanders nipping at her heels, Clinton said she was no longer in favor of the TPP. Charges of flip-flopping and primary progressivism from the Sanders camp ensued (and justifiably so). Either way, the White House's crown jewel in the trade policy realm took a public battering.

* * *

Sanders was still able to differentiate himself from his amorphous opponent, touting his refusal to accept corporate donations and the clear daylight, throughout his career, between himself and Wall Street.

In September, that manifested itself in a challenge to Clinton; to adopt his position on the minimum wage, calling on the former Walmart Boardmember to back an increase to $15/hour. Clinton declined, keeping her proposed increase to $12/hour.

"The current federal minimum wage is a starvation wage, and it must become a living wage," Sanders wrote in a message to supporters. "I believe that position should be adopted by all of the candidates running for president," he added. "Sadly, that is not yet true, even for the Democrats."[53]

But perhaps the most striking contrast between the two candidates on display that month was evident when Sanders went to the hyper-conservative evangelical bastion of Liberty University. Unlike the well-choreographed Clinton campaign (famously photographed in July keeping the press away with a rope perimeter), Sanders' camp was willing—eager, even—to get the candidate out of his comfort zone.

"I understand that the issues of abortion and gay marriage are issues that you feel very strongly about. We disagree on those issues. I get that," Sanders told the crowd. "But let me respectfully suggest that there are other issues out there that are of enormous consequences to our country and the entire world."

From there, he segued into his usual populist message, ruing the 45 million Americans miring in poverty while "the very, very rich become richer."

"That in my view is not justice," he told the students and faculty. "That is a rigged economy, designed by the wealthiest people in this country to benefit the wealthiest people in this country at the expense of everybody else."[54]

The Clinton campaign had received an invite to speak at Liberty University as well, but declined.

* * *

Reinforcing both the palpable need for and the seriousness of Sanders' candidacy, Bernie nabbed some critical endorsements heading into the first Democratic debate in October.

First, one came from those on the frontlines of our still-broken healthcare industry: the 185,000-member National Nurses United. "He's real. He's authentic. That's why we're supporting him," NNU's executive director RoseAnn DeMoro said.[55]

Then, the two co-chairs of the Congressional Progressive Caucus, Reps. Raul Grijalva[56] and Keith Ellison, broke with party leaders to back Sanders.[57] "I couldn't sit on the sidelines and wait for the tea leaves to be read better," Grijalva told *The New York Times*. "The positions he has taken and the values he holds are ones I share." At the time, Sanders had been holding a clear lead over Clinton in critical New Hampshire polls for weeks.[58]

By the time candidates squared off on the debate stage on Oct. 13, Clinton had regained some of the momentum. A challenge from Vice President Joe Biden that could have split party bigwigs never materialized. She also put to rest any lingering doubt surrounding conservatives' obsession with the Sept. 11, 2012 Benghazi Attacks, after weathering a marathon day cross-examination before the House Select Committee looking into the matter.

But when the dust settled after the public tussle, the majority of viewers reported an overwhelming victory for Bernie in online polls (while party establishment pundits took to the television airwaves to claim Clinton had unquestioningly prevailed). By one clear metric, Sanders was the clear winner, nabbing almost 12,000 more Twitter followers than all of the other Democratic candidates put together.[59] The Socialism #Brand was growing.

* * *

By late October, Sanders seemed to revel in the role he was playing—*enfant terrible* trapped in the body of a septuagenarian crank; one imitated on Saturday Night Live that month by comedy legend and fellow Brooklyn Jew, Larry David.

"I don't have a super PAC. I don't even have a backpack," David had said. "I own one pair of underwear."

Sanders replied, noting he has "an ample supply of underwear."

Around the same time, Sanders preempted the quadrennial reefer madness that surrounds presidential politics by calling for marijuana to be fully removed from the DEA schedule of controlled substances, further distinguishing himself from Clinton's regressive record on crime.[60] A month later, her campaign followed suit, sort of, calling for the Devil's Lettuce to be downgraded by the DEA—from a schedule I to a schedule II controlled narcotic.

By then, Sanders candidacy—like his calls for legalization—were hardly beyond the mainstream. He was speaking before audiences swollen with 100,000 people clamoring to hear why America should be more Denmark. In November, he was polling at above 30 percent nationwide.[61]

The socialist was also raising more money than any nominee on the Republican side, becoming the first candidate in US history to receive four million individual contributions. The previous record was held in 2008 by then-Sen. Barack Obama.

By publication, Sanders had won the New Hampshire Primary and drew with Clinton at the Iowa Caucuses. He has promised to take his campaign all the way to the Democratic National Convention in July 2016. It is looking like he'll have a lot of delegates with him, and he might—he just might—win the nomination. Who outside the Senate in April 2015, when Bernie announced his candidacy, would have predicted that?

5. The Long Arm of the Leniency Industrial Complex

Observers could be forgiven for feeling like 2015 was, in many respects, similar to the years that preceded it; in that nothing was done to stop systemic police violence in America.

A running study by *The Guardian* found late in the year that unarmed victims of fatal police violence were 1.5 times more likely to be black than white; and that cops killed well over three Americans every day, overall, throughout the year.[62] What gave protests and disturbances in Ferguson, Mo. immediate support throughout the country in August 2014 was still undeniably true last year: there were Michael Browns everywhere throughout the United States and their killings were practically foreseeable, on the macro level.

There appeared, however, the emergence of a major shift appearing in Washington. The idea that police, perhaps, shouldn't be encouraged (tacitly or otherwise) to act like Falangist paramilitaries began to gain currency in Washington, for the first time since the Reagan Administration, when the War on Drugs was ramped up to its current heightened state.

In **MAY**, for example, President Obama forbade the Pentagon from granting a wide variety of military assets to local police departments. The deployment of heavily armored vehicles and high caliber weaponry against protesters in Ferguson—both the peaceful and the marginally-militant— had shocked a nation unused to seeing its ugliest side broadcast on cable primetime. The White House therefore decided to cut off cops from unneeded DOD tanks, weaponized aircraft, grenade launchers, bayonets, .50 caliber-plus ammunition, and camo uniforms, declaring the provisions "inconsistent with the premise of civilian law enforcement."[63]

And later in the year, House and Senate Committees agreed upon proposals to reduce draconian federal mandatory minimum prison sentences—key buttresses of Drug War enforcement.

As of publication, they hadn't even yet received a full chamber vote, in either house. But the bipartisan agreements were themselves something of an achievement. Republicans largely conceded crucial ideological ground, effectively admitting that decades of law-and-order veneration had failed to produce a result Washington should be proud of—the world's largest prison population just doesn't sound great at embassy cocktail parties.

* * *

In February, *The New York Times* helped get the ball rolling, describing Senate Judiciary Committee chair Chuck Grassley (R-Iowa) as a "roadblock" to the relaxation of mandatory minimums. The paper noted wide bipartisan support for the move, but Grassley, it said, "for reasons that defy basic fairness and empirical data, has remained an opponent of almost any reduction of those sentences."[64]

In early March, Grassley responded by lashing out at The Gray Lady—and his colleagues—from the floor of the senate, casting them as rubes. He said reformers were captured by a "leniency industrial complex," and living in an "Orwellian World."

"Problems do exist in the criminal justice system. I plan to use the Judiciary Committee to address some important ones," he remarked. "But rather than marking up ill-considered and dangerous legislation like the so-called Smarter Sentencing Act, we will take up bills that can achieve a large measure of consensus."[65]

Behind the scenes, over the coming months, the bipartisan bedfellowship would chip away at Grassley's siege mentality—aided, perhaps, by a gruesome homicide that amplified calls for reform.

When it emerged that police in Baltimore killed another innocent black man named Freddie Gray—by, according to city prosecutors, illegally detaining him then driving recklessly with the 25-year-old unsecured in the back of a van (a "rough ride," in local cop talk)—the city exploded in protest. Some it wasn't peaceful. If disturbances in a small town like Ferguson bothered a nation that sometimes sees itself as "post-racial," the images from Baltimore and details of the killing that preceded them truly disturbed it at its bones.

"To see [Baltimore] erupt into violence underscored the urgent need to examine systemic problems facing our criminal justice system at its core," Charm City resident Elijah Cummings (D-Md.) said in July, as ranking member of the House oversight committee.

As it was in the Senate, the call resonated across the aisle. "One of the more impactful things I did as a member of Congress was to go visit Congressman Cummings' district," committee chair Jason Chaffetz (R-Utah) said at the same hearing.

Chaffetz recalled a meeting with former inmates who told him about the reality of trying to eke out a legal living upon returning from prison. "They had been convicted and sentenced, and served those sentences, but now had a hard time getting out of that box," he remarked. "You're a 22 year-old male with a felony on your record. What are you supposed to do?"

"How are you supposed to get a job?" he continued. "You wanna right your life, you paid your debt to society, then what do you do? We better address that if we wanna make this country the premier country that I know that it is."[66]

The same month, *The Hill* reported Grassley agreed to legislate "some reductions" to mandatory minimums.[67] By October, a bill was finalized. The chair rolled it out in a press briefing, with his committee members behind him; their spat, water under the bridge.

"It's a product of a very thoughtful bipartisan deliberation by the Congress," Grassley said in a press conference. "There are things in here that each of us like. There are items that each of us would rather do without. But this is how the process works here in Congress."[68]

As promised, reformers were left with reservations. ACLU executive director Anthony Romero said the organization has "deep concerns" about the raising of some mandatory minimums. Families Against Mandatory Minimums president Julie Stewart did too, befitting of her organization's name.[69]

"It's a shame that some lawmakers have not broken their addiction to mandatory minimums despite mountains of evidence proving they aren't necessary or proven to deter crime," she said.

But, as the pair both recognized, most of the Drug War's legislative weaponry had, previously, been untouchable. Stewart said it was "the most significant pieces of sentencing reform legislation in a generation." Romero called it "promising."

In November, after the House Judiciary Committee advanced its version of the bill, another advocate for reform, Drug Policy Alliance deputy director Michael Collins characterized both votes as "historic."

"We have a bill moving in the Senate, and now we have a companion bill moving in the House, so I'm optimistic we'll have legislation on the President's desk in a matter of months," he said.[70]

* * *

The prospect of substantially beating back the American police state was always rather grim, however, if its acute sensitivity to criticism was any indication. The Bureau that J.Edgar Hoover Built, for example, scrambled surveillance aircraft over Baltimore during the Freddie Gray upheaval, the White House admitted in early May.[71]

The problem wasn't that the feds were monitoring a local disturbance from above, but rather that entire communities had reason to believe they were being intimately watched, given what we know about US domestic aerial surveillance capabilities. Late in 2014 year, it had been revealed the FBI and local police departments use cell phone tower simulators known as "stingrays" to collect bulk data on Americans from above, without first obtaining a warrant.

Those suspicions were not assuaged in June, when an AP report revealed that the FBI was, in fact, flying stingrays over American cities, including Baltimore, and that the operations hadn't been preceded by a warrant.

The Bureau denied that it was part of a "secret" program, however, and defended the flights as enabling "operations security," not "mass surveillance."[72]

"If there is tremendous turbulence in a community, it's useful to everybody—civilians and law enforcement—to have a view of what's going on," FBI Director Comey explained in October. "Where are the fires in this community? Where are people gathering? Where do people need help?"[73]

Federal intelligence gatherers' version of "community help," however, might not exactly comport with on-the-ground working definitions. In August, *Vice News'* Jason Leopold revealed, via FOIA requests, that the Department of Homeland Security had been tracking nationally prominent Black Lives Matter organizer and Twitter personality Deray McKesson—a fact made more troubling by McKesson's occasional online meandering to laud fairly establishment-friendly commodities, such as charter schools and various snacks.

"[S]ocial media monitors have reported that a professional demonstrator/protester known to law enforcement (Deray Mckesson) has posts on his social media account that there is going to be a 3:00 pm rally" for Freddie Gray in Baltimore, the dossier revealed.[74]

Rest assured, City of Baltimore, the United States knows where the fires in you community are: they're organizing citizens to tell police that it's wrong to murder black people. There might even be tweets about Doritos and Teach for America being good.

The federal status of cannabis, too, continued to lord over the heads of many Americans—particularly those without white skin. Though Congress failed to stop Washington, D.C. from legalizing it early in 2015, in many ways official attitudes remained regressive. The acting head of the DEA, Chuck Rosenberg even described medicinal marijuana as a "joke," saying the plant was "bad and dangerous"—like some PSA from the nineteen fucking fifties. And when asked why the agency still considers cannabis to be as dangerous as heroin, meth, and cocaine, Attorney General Loretta Lynch claimed that we simply still don't know enough.

"With respect to the issue of scheduling, that is typically determined based on whether or not there is another use for the product," Lynch attempted to explain, to Rep. Stephen Cohen (D-Tenn.) in November. "And I think there would have to be studies by the FDA among others to determine whether or not a scheduling change in any drug is necessary." ("You have to change the scheduling from one to get the studies," Cohen snapped back.)[75]

Additionally looming over Americans (again, particularly those of color): the idea that scrutiny of the police itself threatened the social order. Reactionary types claimed that a "Ferguson Effect" had caused an outbreak of shyness among cops; a phenomenon, they said, that resulted in a nationwide crime-wave.

"Cops across this country are feeling the assault," Ted Cruz (R-Texas) said in September. "They're feeling the assault from the President, from the top on down as we see. Whether it's in Ferguson or Baltimore, the response of senior officials of the President, of the Attorney General, is to vilify law enforcement."[76]

Though the White House was somewhat sympathetic to protesters, not all members of the administration held the line, with some buying into the Ferguson Effect theory. "A chill wind has blown through law enforcement over the last year, and that wind is surely changing behavior," James

Comey said in October.[77] Although he later admitted he had no statistics to back up this theory, Comey stuck by his guns, calling his conclusion "common sense." Chuck "Marijuana Is Bad and Dangerous" Rosenberg followed suit in November, directly endorsing the FBI chief's statements. Both men were publicly rebuked by Josh Earnest.[78]

"Mr. Rosenberg, as you pointed out, is the second administration official to make that kind of claim without any evidence," Earnest told a reporter who asked. "I guess you'd have to ask him exactly what point he's trying to make. You might also ask him if there's any evidence to substantiate the claim that he's made."[79]

* * *

Indeed, it would have been news to Black Americans that police were toning it down—as mentioned, over one thousand people in the US were killed by police in 2015; hundreds were unarmed, a disproportionate number, people of color.

One young Black American who lost her life after an encounter with cops was Sandra Bland. The 28-year-old black activist and college professor was found hanging in her jail cell in July, days after being roughed up while being arrested during a routine traffic stop. Texas State Trooper Brian Encinia screamed at Bland that he would drag her out of her car, at one point yelling "I will light you up."

"You're a real man now, you just slammed me, knocked my head into the ground. I got epilepsy, you motherfucker," Bland said, according to the audio from publicly-released dashcam footage. "Good" was Encinia's reply.[80] Local officials ruled her death days later a suicide. They changed tack after a public outcry and launched an investigation into the matter. As did the FBI. In December, however, a grand jury at the county level declined to find anyone criminally liable for Bland's death.[81]

The Justice Department didn't bother opening its own probe into the incident, despite pleas from Bland's sister[82] and some Congressional Black

Caucus members. "A person who is stopped for a minor traffic violation should not end up dead," Rep. Al Green (D-Texas) said. "This is what the Justice Department is for: to look into these questionable circumstances, of which too many have occurred as of late and, quite frankly, over a substantial period of time in our country."[83]

A few days after the Bland no-bill, a similar panel in Cleveland declined to indict Timothy Loehmann, the cop who, the year before, fatally shot Tamir Rice—a 12-year-old child who was playing in a park with a toy gun.[84]

It was the same fate that had met Michael Brown's assailant, former Ferguson police officer Darren Wilson, two days after Rice's killing. Tragically, one can expect dozens of similar slaughters to go unpunished in into 2016 and beyond, whether or not they receive nationwide attention.

6. "Broken Promises"

Barack Obama might come to regret branding the Trans Pacific Partnership as "the most progressive trade deal in history."[85] A meaningless distinction from inception (the WTO and NAFTA set low benchmarks), Congressional Dems disputed the talking point in 2015 to devastating effect. As a result of their prodding from the left, the TPP looks far more in doubt than it ought to at this stage.

While many Dems on Capitol Hill can claim credit for this development, few are as deserving of it as Sen. Sherrod Brown (D-Ohio). In the Spring, as Congress debated a must-pass procedure—Trade Promotion Authority, or the "fast-track" bill—Brown filed 88 amendments; one for every county in his Rust Belt State. Some were decried as "poison pills" by the administration. The senator did not dispute the characterization.[86]

In **JUNE**, he fumed from the Senate floor that the TPP might impact laws aimed at curbing smoking, but that Congress didn't even know if this was even the case. While it was being hammered out, negotiating parties kept the working text under tight lock-and-key; a routine source of grievance among Democratic Caucus members. "Even something this clearly violative of the public interest and of public health as the damage big tobacco inflicts on children—even that is not, to our knowledge being addressed," Brown said.[87]

Though the scraggly-voiced senator sounds like he himself hacks through two dozen Marlboro Reds every night (at least), Brown appeared to have struck a nerve. In July, a number of Dems on the House Ways and Means Committee wrote to USTR Michael Froman, charging that the public interest was under siege "from tobacco industry subversion in the TPP."[88] Whatever the impact, the US delegation pushed through the final agreement provisions barring tobacco companies from accessing TPP dispute resolution tribunals.

It might not have been Dems' intention, but some Republicans greeted this modest proposal by proverbially strapping dynamite to their chests. Rather than accept what they saw as the good with the bad, the North Carolina senate delegation acted like the shutting out of Joe Camel was analogous to Jim Crow. Sens. Thom Tillis (R-N.C.) and Richard Burr (R-N.C.) denounced the move, with the former promising to both vote and whip against it.[89]

"It's ironic that the idea of equal treatment and due process is being peddled with our trading partners as equal treatment and due process for everyone but some members of the minority," Tillis said in July, as rumors of the "carve-out" surfaced. "You may feel comfortable that this could never happen to you; to a sector in your state's economy. But I believe you should be worried."[90] First, they came for the Philip Morris lawyers.

These egalitarian concerns reverberated to the top of the GOP Senate hierarchy. Majority Leader Mitch McConnell (R-Ky.) asked the president to refrain from targeting "a specific US agriculture commodity — in this case tobacco."[91] Finance Committee Chair Orrin Hatch (R-Utah) told NPR that "as much as I hate tobacco, we needed to have it in there."[92] Hatch noted fast-track only cleared the cloture-filibuster hurdle by three votes.

What made Republican leaders so glum is that Democrats barely flinched at news of the carve-out. Brown had called for the outright elimination of the TPP mediation tribunals in question; investor-state dispute settlement (ISDS) panels. Critics have decried existing ISDSs created under past deals as opaque courts, noting their power to award investors (and only investors) large sums of money if governments don't grant them "minimum standards of treatment."[93] Brown said the tobacco amendment merely represented "true progress on that issue."[94]

Sen. Richard Blumenthal (D-Conn.), meanwhile, gleefully pointed out how the exemption highlighted "dangers posed both by tobacco and by [ISDS]." The same boards that can't be entrusted to oversee a single product with widely-known side effects are expected, apparently, to dutifully uphold the integrity of financial safeguards, workplace safety and public health regulations, copyright law, and whole range of other matters.[95]

* * *

If the carve-out can be taken as an admission by the White House that the TPP framework should give progressives some concern, it came as something of a surprise. The administration insisted that the agreement framework was fundamentally geared toward opening avenues between consumers and producers.

"[W]e think market access is an appropriate issue to be negotiated in trade negotiations," Treasury Secretary Lew remarked in March. "Prudential standards," he said, were not subject to "trade negotiating processes or trade remedies."[96]

Where "market access" ends and regulatory matters begin in the TPP, however, is blurred; almost intentionally so, in light of its focus on "non-tariff barriers"—or "laws," as people without advanced economics degrees might call them. Like in January, for instance, when Froman assured Republicans he was in favor of data localization bans called for by Wall Street—an initiative that could effectively hamstring regulators on the beat.[97]

The general cognitive dissonance lit a fire under liberal legislators in colorful ways reminiscent of a pre-2009 Washington.

"Perhaps [Froman] has gotten access under DC's new legalization law to some marijuana and he's filling in gaps in his memory with confabulated facts," Rep. Peter DeFazio (D-Ore.) said in March. Rep. Mark Pocan (D-Wis.) told reporters that Froman's case for TPP involved "baffling them with bullshit."[98] By April, the administration was relenting on some of the secrecy shrouding negotiations, granting lawmakers a chance to review "an unredacted version" of the working text. Rep. Alan Grayson (D-Florida) told *The Sentinel* it was "a very passive aggressive concession."

"They're losing votes," Grayson said. "Members are saying in meetings 'why are you playing these games with us? We have a constitutional duty to review these agreements.'"[99]

But no interaction between the legislative and executive highlighted Barack Obama's inability to connect with his base on this issue like his May rebuke of Elizabeth Warren. Obama said the progressive firebrand did not pass "the test of fact and scrutiny" when she panned his trade agenda as a gift to Corporate America. A week later, the senator's office issued a 15-page, 68-footnote response called "Broken Promises."[100]

"President Obama has repeatedly stated that the TPP is 'the most progressive trade bill in history,'" the report stated. "But proponents of almost every free trade agreement (FTA) in the last 20 years have made virtually identical claims."

The report's chronicling of US trade partners running roughshod over workers post-liberalization, in particular, did not make for comforting reading. Of the twenty countries that have entered into FTAs with the United States, Warren staffers cited "significant problems with use of child labor or other labor-related human rights abuses in eleven."[101]

Thus, after the deal was finalized in October and released in November, there were few surprises—though Rep. Louise Slaughter (D-N.Y.) took aim at privacy measures in a tweet with the hashtag: #TPPWorseThanWeThought.[102] Congressional Progressive Caucus co-chair Keith Ellison said that "Americans can see for themselves whose interests are prioritized when a trade deal is negotiated in secret with unprecedented input from multinational corporations."

He took exception to how the agreement would deregulate the economy in every way possible—except where it cracks down on copyright infringement. "The TPP is not progressive," Ellison said. "It is a bad deal for working families."[103]

* * *

It is a lasting tribute to Washington's cynicism then that TPP might die not because it is "a bad deal for working families" but because it wouldn't grant rights to tobacco companies.

Conservatives and liberals on Capitol Hill, after all, could unite behind an alleged Executive Branch fraud that, if true, made a mockery of them both and called into disrepute a regular foreign policy assessment that still carries significance abroad: the State Department's Trafficking In Persons (TIP) report.

When the fast-track/trade promotion authority bill passed in the Spring, Sen. Bob Menendez managed to attach to it a provision declaring countries with a "Tier 3" TIP rating ineligible for the TPP. The measure was aimed squarely at Malaysia, a TPP negotiating partner and Tier 3-designee for many of the preceding years, including 2014. But when the 2015 report came out, State concluded Malaysia belonged in Tier 2.[104] An investigation published by Reuters not long after uncovered "a degree of intervention not previously known by diplomats in a report that can lead to sanctions and is the basis for many countries' anti-trafficking policies." The meddling impacted rankings of fourteen "strategically important countries." Malaysia was among them.[105]

The Senate Foreign Relations Committee took note, and, generally speaking, wasn't pleased. Its chair, Bob Corker (R-Tenn.), called one State official's defense of the report "heartless" and repeatedly threatened to subpoena the department for internal TIP records.[106] One of those threats came in September after a classified briefing by Deputy Secretary of State Tony Blinken. An informational session, Corker said, that left him "very unsatisfied."[107]

In November, the committee's House counterpart pressed on for answers in a separate hearing, featuring State's TIP office chair, Dr. Kari Johnstone. Both Republican and Democratic members were left wanting to go further up the ladder.

"As we started to do the analysis about who was included and who was excluded, it appears that it goes to the very highest levels within the State Department in them weighing in on who should be on the report and who should not," Rep. Mark Meadows (R-N.C.) said at the top of the set piece. Another aggrieved lawmaker, Rep. Brad Sherman, said it was "why the Secretary of State ought to have the whatevers to come before Congress and defend this decision."[108]

It never seemed likely, however, that lawmakers would use the effective usurpation of their authority to pull the rug out from under the TPP.

"As much as I might disagree, I would be more respectful of the competing interests saying: 'Look, we need Malaysia in the Trans Pacific Partnership," Menendez said in September. "We think that's important for our Pivot to Asia. I might disagree with that, but at least I respect that."[109]

Either way, those who have been hoping for TPP's death won't care how it happens, if it does, when McConnell brings the deal up for a vote late in 2016, as he is expected to. If TPP crumbles due to the fallout over the whitewashing of systemic human rights abuses or due to tobacco company lobbying, the end result would be the same.

It would bring the administration's "most progressive trade deal in history" talking point closer in line with both the Democratic Party base and the truth: the most progressive free trade agreement in history, at this point, would absolutely be a failed one.

7. Out of Oversight, Out of Mind

In the first week of 2015, the Obama administration gambled on a Syria strategy, confident of its ability to enact regime change in the Middle East with more sleight of hand than long arm—a deliberate contrast to the approach preferred by its predecessor.

With $500 million from Congress, the Pentagon deployed four hundred US troops to neighboring countries to raise a 15,000 strong army of moderate Syrian rebels; one that would be enlisted in a multi-front civil war against the Islamic State in Iraq and Syria (ISIL) and forces loyal to Bashar al Assad (who, in case you weren't aware, were and still are also fighting each other).[110]

By the summer, all signs were pointing to failure. The Defense Department revised down its goal of training 5,000 fighters by the end of the year to 3,000. And in, **JULY**, in testimony before the Senate Armed Services Committee, Defense Secretary Ash Carter made those already reined-in expectations seem like a pipe dream.

"This number is much smaller than we hoped for at this point," he admitted. Six months into the mission, US military advisors were training only sixty Syrian fighters—an entire busload of warriors. "That's not a very impressive number," committee chair John McCain replied.[111]

The administration had prepared explanations (sort of). Carter chalked up the low numbers to the stringent vetting standards. Gen. Martin Dempsey hypothesized that Ramadan observations, which had began the previous month, may have also been dragging down recruitment numbers. "There's a lot of folks that are interested in being with their families during that period," the Joint Chief of Staffs chair told reporters, during a July press briefing. "We may see after Ramadan that some of the ones we lost may come back." They never did.[112]

In September, the committee would learn that the entire program had only produced "four or five" Syrian fighters ready for battle. "It's time for a new plan," Sen. Claire McCaskill (D-Mo.) told Pentagon officials in response.[113]

A month later, the $500 million gambit was scrapped; or at least significantly narrowed to focus on leadership training. Putting the nail in the coffin was the Russian Air Force, which launched a devastating bombing campaign in support of the Assad government; pummeling areas controlled by rebels, both extremist and moderate factions (with noticeably less precision than the US-led anti-ISIL coalition, according to observers). It would have been unfair to expect some kind of paradigm-shifting response from the five Syrians willing to take to the battlefield with the help of the US government.

* * *

It also would have been unfair to mention "willingness" and the counter-ISIL campaign's shortcomings in 2015 without chronicling how the legislative branch oversaw the war—or, rather, how it didn't. While the missions in Syria and Iraq crept along, Congress took little interest in actually signing off on them, despite its constitutional mandate to "provide for the common Defense...of the United States."

In February, the White House dropped a proposed Authorization for the Use of Military Force (AUMF) against ISIL, but it was received coldly—even by its natural allies.[114] Hawks argued it was too restrictive and unnecessary, even, as long as the post 9/11 AUMF was still on the books. The administration had been citing the law as legitimating the war—launched almost thirteen years after the Twin Towers came down.

"Let me be crystal clear: we didn't start this. We're not about to start a third war," John Kerry said in late 2014. "Osama Bin Laden started this on 9/11 in 2001, and he has continued it, in absentia, obviously."[115]

That answer hadn't sat well with many in his own party. "Those of use who were in Congress in 2001 never envisioned that authorization would

51

still be utilized today the way it was utilized in thirty separate military operations," Sen. Ben Cardin (D-Md.) noted later. "We were interested in going after those who attacked our country on Sept. 11."

But still, the Authorization went nowhere while the Use of Military Force continued unabated. Critics from the Right were happy to rely on the administration's backward-looking justification—particularly if that meant avoiding a sensitive roll call vote. Critics from the Left, meanwhile, seemed most concerned with limiting and managing the Pentagon—not stopping it from acting altogether.

To up the ante, the administration admitted in 2015 that it had deployed ground forces to Syria (albeit in an limited capacity), contra President Obama's pledge to avoid putting "boots on the ground" there. During testimony before the Senate Armed Services Committee in September, CENTCOM chief Gen. Lloyd Austin claimed US special forces were "at the very outset" working with counter-ISIL fighters like the Syrian Kurdish YPG.[116] And throughout 2015, US special forces were routinely moving against Islamic State targets in both Iraq and Syria; raiding leadership hideouts and freeing hostages, in often intense firefights. An American soldier was killed in one such mission in Iraq at the end of October.

The stakes of the air campaign itself were already high enough. By the end of 2015, US and coalition forces launched more than 9,800 airstrikes against ISIL targets in both Syria and Iraq, according to Airwars.org, a non-profit transparency project monitoring the war. The group estimated that between 833 and 2,589 civilians had been killed the bombing raids.

The US military, however, only confirmed 16 civilian deaths by publication, after investigating 120 incidents—roughly one-third of the number of fatal incidents documented by Airwars, using open source investigation.[117]

Maybe Congress will look into the matter if it decides to retroactively authorize the airstrikes. It might still get a chance, perhaps under a new administration. At the start of 2016, the Islamic State still held the majority of territory it occupied the year before, including Raqqa, its *de facto* capital in Syria, and Mosul, an Iraqi city of roughly 2.5 million people before it was first taken over by ISIL, in June 2014.

* * *

The properly overseen war—the one in Afghanistan—was not devoid of its own foibles in 2015; well documented in both lengthy reports and shocking headlines. Doing some of the most diligent work, as far as the former was concerned, was John Sopko, the Special Inspector General for Afghanistan Reconstruction (SIGAR).

The $100 billion nation building effort—nearly as old as the longest running war itself—was pried open by Sopko in several scathing probes chronicling waste on an enormous scale by various Pentagon, State Department, and USAID acronyms (and their Afghan counterparts).

In March, SIGAR warned of declining troop numbers in the Afghan National Army (ANA). Although the Department of Defense had invested more than $33 billion in building up the fighting force since the start of the war, Sopko reported that "attrition continues to be a major challenge." He noted tens of thousands of fighters had "dropped from ANA rolls" in the previous twelve months. "Afghan self-sustainment of its security institutions is long way away," he said in a May speech. He added that the forces "will need our help for the foreseeable future."[118]

SIGAR also teased out gritty details of the failed $8 billion counternarcotics operations that hasn't seemed to even put a dent in Afghanistan's poppy yields. "Afghan farmers are growing more opium than ever before," Sopko noted.

In May, his office documented just who had been benefiting throughout the debacle. Notably, the company contracted second most by the Defense Department was Academi—the private security firm formally known as Blackwater: an entity whose most known contribution to history, as of publication, was a 2007 massacre in Baghdad that left 17 Iraqi civilians dead. Between 2002 and 2013, US taxpayers were billed $309 million for Afghan counter-narcotics operations by this rebranded synonym of Bush-era scandal (Northrup Grumman raked in the most, collecting $325 million).[119] In the same time frame, Afghanistan's opium production almost doubled, increasing to about 5,500 from 3,400 tons.[120]

But the dirtiest nuggets Sopko dug up in 2015 involved an obscure, shadowy business liaison set up by the Pentagon to encourage private investment in countries it leveled. Called the Task Force for Business and Stability Operations (TFBSO), the economic development arm had its origins in George W. Bush's Iraqi quagmire. In the first year of the Obama administration, it set up shop in Afghanistan and spared no expense.

Sopko first unveiled that the task force built a compressed natural gas station that ultimately cost $43 million—roughly $42.5 million over-budget.[121] More jarringly, his office also found the TFBSO sunk $150 million on lavish villas and private security forces for only a handful of employees.[122]

Congress ordered the task force to close up shop in Afghanistan at the end of 2014, amid a significant troop reduction. By then, it had spent more than $638 million in the impoverished nation. The fact that the TFBSO no longer existed was another excuse for the Pentagon to stonewall Sopko's probe. He called it "one of the most troubling aspects" of the entire affair; though he might be able to get to the bottom of the matter before the war ends.[123]

* * *

The troubles facing Afghanistan's economy and US nation-building efforts seemed to pale in comparison to the deteriorating security situation there. By the end of 2015, the Taliban controlled about three-tenths of the country—more territory than it had taken since the US first ousted the group in 2001.

In the autumn, there was one extraordinarily horrific direct American contribution to the chaos. On Oct. 3, a US gunship launched an hour-long attack on a Doctors Without Borders (MSF) facility in the city of Kunduz—a center of fierce fighting between Taliban insurgents and US-supported Afghan soldiers. The sustained assault on the clinic left 22 civilians dead, including medical staff and patients.

The details of the attack were no less shocking than the length and scale of the bombing. "One MSF staff member described a patient in a wheelchair attempting to escape from the inpatient department when he was killed by shrapnel from a blast," the NGO said in an investigation published in November. "An MSF doctor suffered a traumatic amputation to the leg in one of the blasts," it continued, describing another casualty. "He was later operated on by the MSF team on a make-shift operating table on an office desk where he died."[124]

The Pentagon's explanation for the slaughter had itself been no small disaster. The military, after changing its story twice, claimed that Afghan forces had called for US air support at a location where Taliban fighters were allegedly taking cover, and that several civilians were "accidentally" killed as a result. Doctors Without Borders promptly replied by calling the story a war crime confession.[125]

"These statements imply that Afghan and US forces working together decided to raze to the ground a fully functioning hospital–with more than 180 staff and patients inside–because they claim that members of the Taliban were present," the group said in a statement.

Defense officials later altered their alibi, saying Afghan allies didn't communicate any info on targeting, and that the hospital was mistakenly struck. Gen. John Campbell, the commander of US troops in Afghanistan, told the Senate Armed Services Committee just days later that "we would never intentionally target a protected medical facility.

The Associated Press reported two weeks later, however, that US special forces had been watching the facility in the days leading up to the attack—

well aware of the medical site's protected status, while suspecting it of harboring insurgents. [126]

In its November report, Doctors Without Borders bolstered this story. It recounted US military officials contacting its Kunduz clinic on Oct. 1 to ask if a large number of Taliban fighters were "holed up" inside. MSF replied that they were, indeed, treating Taliban fighters, with the war raging all around the city, but that neither they nor the government forces that were also being treated there were in violation of the hospital's disarmament policy.

"What we know is that we were running a hospital treating patients, including wounded combatants from both sides–this was not a 'Taliban base,'" MSF President Joanne Liu said. The White House has repeatedly denied the organization's request to allow an independent inquiry into the massacre.

Not long after flattening the only hospital in a city of nearly 270,000 people, President Obama did, however, decide it was too soon to withdraw US troops from Afghanistan. The administration had planned to remove all but a thousand-strong embassy protection force out of the country by the end of 2016. But following military gains by the Taliban throughout the year—in places like Kunduz, which it had temporarily seized—he reversed course.

The President announced on Oct. 15 that he will maintain the size of the current Afghan contingency (nearly 10,000 troops) through most of 2016, and that roughly 5,000 troops would stay in Afghanistan into 2017.[127] The scope of the mission then will be something for the next administration to decide, keeping the meter running indefinitely on the longest war in American history.

8. "A Lot of Risky Business"

If fighting corporate rule in Washington sometimes overwhelms progressives, they can take comfort in one fact: even the most mild of reforms inspire theatrical pants-shitting on the right.

In **AUGUST**, for example, after the SEC[ix] passed a rule requiring companies listed on the stock exchange to reveal CEO compensation relative to median pay, a Republican member of the SEC described the move as ushering in a new era of anti-capitalism. In his dissent, Commisioner Michael Piwowar said the rule smacked of "Saul Alinskyan tactics" and grander machinations.

"Nearly fifteen years ago, Big Labor supporters published a book called *Working Capital: The Power of Labor's Pensions* that contained a strategy to re-make the capital markets with a so-called 'worker-owner' viewpoint," he explained. "The worker-owner approach would aim to 'inject workers' welfare, broadly understood, into investment priorities'...and principles that guide capital allocation.'"[128]

Labor organizers could be forgiven for admiring Piwowar, for seemingly believing that a bit of transparency will yield Full Communism, when even the most minor of leftish achievements in the US typically result from Sisyphean toil (and only after right-wing catastrophe).

The truth is that the CEO Pay Ratio rule, more than anything, exemplified Wall Street's handle on the United States government. The SEC had been ordered to make the rule about a half-decade before, by Dodd-Frank financial reform. It might have floated eternally in regulatory purgatory but for a bit of "name and shame" in the Senate.

In June, Sen. Elizabeth Warren had written to SEC Chair Mary Jo White

---

[ix]   Securities and Exchange Commission

demanding to know why White said in a previous meeting that the rule would be finalized "by fall" on the same day that the White House later said it would be ready in April 2016.

"I am perplexed as to how and why you would have provided me with this misinformation," Warren said, claiming "there could not have been a misunderstanding."[129] Eight weeks later, a final rule was adopted.[130] No means of production were seized in the aftermath.

* * *

As already alluded to, the vast majority of pressure on the financial regulatory regime in 2015 was coming from the industry. After Republicans took back the Senate and control of both chambers for the first time since 2006, they attempted to enact all sorts of Dodd-Frank roll-backs. But the biggest and most successful push actually came just after the 2014 midterm.

Backed by a lobbying initiative led, in part, by Citigroup and JP Morgan CEO Jamie Dimon (who personally phoned lawmakers), conservatives proposed exempting vast quantities of derivatives trades from a Dodd-Frank rule that was set to take effect in 2015. Section 716—the so-called "Prohibition against Federal Government bailouts of swaps entities"—was written to limit the types of speculative trades that can be made with consumer savings, which are guaranteed by the federal government. The idea behind the regulation was to diminish private risk with nationalized insurance. It didn't stand a chance.

During end-of-the-year budget haggling that coincided with yet more GOP government shutdown threats, the "swaps pushout" was attached to must-pass legislation. Sen. Warren whipped for a "no vote" on the package, denouncing it as a deregulatory Trojan Horse. She nearly succeeded, but the "cromnibus" was carried by the Wall Street wing of the Democratic Party, squeaking through the House by thirteen votes.[x]

---

[x] A great number of the Dems who carried it, it should be noted, were among the party's top

Warren, however, wouldn't soon forget the treachery. After a lengthy investigation, she and Rep. Elijah Cummings estimated in November 2015 that the repeal kept $10 trillion worth of derivatives trades tied to public guarantees. Warren called it "a lot of risky business" from the Senate floor. "The whole TARP bailout was less than $1 trillion," she said.

Warren also noted that Citigroup, Dimon's JP Morgan Chase, and Bank of America were found to have been "gobbling down most of this $10 trillion in risk."[131] Whoever points to the myriad debt ceiling crises to say that nothing got done in Washington under Speaker Boehner (see Chapter Ten) is besmirching the good name of Wall Street lobbyists.

* * *

Underpinning anxiety about the swaps push-out were fears—not since assuaged—that another massive financial calamity is far from being out of the question. In late 2014, a Treasury Department research arm created after the crisis identified potential systemic pitflls. Inadequate collateral across-the-board could lead to a credit crunch in the event of a downturn, the Office of Financial Research (OFR) warned. In other words, Very Serious People were somewhat concerned about loads of investors getting caught in a pinch with their pants around their ankles, as they had in a big way in 2008.

To that end, OFR also fretted about more and more economic activity gravitating toward "difficult to assess" sectors since the collapse. "Assets under management have increased ten-fold over the last five years, driven by a search for yield and a hedge against an eventual rise in interest rates," it said. The trend led to risk being "concentrated in non-bank entities that are not directly regulated by banking supervisors" (i.e. hedge funds, asset managers, and Exchange-Traded Funds).[132]

In the summer of 2015, concerns about stability flared up in Washington;

beneficiaries of JP Morgan and Citibank campaign donations.

at least for a few news cycles. On Aug. 24, a nosedive by the stock market in Shanghai spread panic throughout the world—first in Europe, then on this side of the Atlantic. Key indices in Frankfurt, Madrid, Paris, and London shed about five cents on the dollar that day. As New Yorkers drank their morning cawffees, the Dow Jones Industrial Average (DJIA), the S&P 500 and the NASDAQ Indexes all started having a serious case of the runs.

The White House, however, seemed confident about its approach to the whole thing. Josh Earnest, on the same day, encouraged reporters to "take a look at the impact of Wall Street reform legislation."

"US banks have reduced their leverage and added $600 billion in capital since 2009," he said. "Some of that is related to new requirements under Wall Street reform. Banks are less reliant on unstable short-term funding, and they're better able to withstand short-term volatility in financial markets."[133]

Speaking over the White House Press Secretary Earnest, however, were nosediving markets. The DJIA shed 3 percent of its value by the end of the day—the eighth worst in its history, in absolute terms. By the middle of the week, the sell-off saw $2.1 trillion in wealth evaporate.[134]

OFR took note of the tumult in its 2015 annual report. The "macroeconomic risk" to the United States, it said, was "moderate," but "elevated and rising" in certain sectors, with "deterioration concentrated in emerging markets."[135] More bad news about the troubled Chinese economy could inflict serious pain on this side of the Pacific, with our highly financialized system bound to magnify the problem.

If that comes in 2016, Earnest might not be so quick to cite President Obama's impact on the financial sector—unless, by then, he is working for the Bernie Sanders campaign and posting a teary *mea culpa* on Medium (see Chapter Four).

* * *

The administration, to its credit, did in 2015 seek to get ahead of some problems. But in one major case, it was after markets had already exposed regulators as being behind the curve.

On Oct. 15, 2014, Treasury bond yields fluctuated in what was their fourth most volatile trading day since 1998 (like 2008, a year synonymous with worldwide instability). The violent swing had particularly troubled global economic gatekeepers because Treasury bonds are widely seen as safe bets, and because it had happened in the absence of a major news event. In OFR's words: there was a "lack of a significant fundamental driver."[136] It wasn't exactly something that could be explained by an ECON101 professor.

A year later, the CFTC[xi] responding by proposing safeguards on computerized trading, including High-Frequency Trading. A cross-agency investigation published in the summer had found algorithmic transactions featured heavily in the Oct. 15 "flash." CFTC Chair Tim Massad pointed out that many other increasingly automated markets seemed to be increasingly "irrational" in similar ways.

"In just this year, for example, there were about 35 events meeting this [Oct. 15] definition [of "flash" volatility] involving the [West Texas Index] crude oil contract," Massad said. He noted flash days were also quite common in corn, gold and other commodity markets. "In fact corn, the largest grain futures market, averaged more than five such events per year over the last five years." he remarked.[137] In November, the CFTC got started on the lengthy rule-making process, on "malfunctioning algorithms."[138]

The SEC, too, vowed to apply tougher regulatory standards to a sector of the financial sector that had gotten ahead of it—the asset management industry (the very same that troubled OFR). Mary Jo White, in November, said asset managers would soon be subject to stress tests, living wills, and

---

xi   Commodity Futures Trading Commission

additional rules on derivatives trades.[139]

That the outcome of these rules are still very much in doubt does not bode well for those concerned that the United States failed to learn the lessons of the last catastrophe. The administration's refusal to disavow hands-off regulation surfaced throughout 2015—like when global financial regulators declined to name the largest asset managers in the world "systemically important," shadowing a move made by the Obama admin the year before.[140]

White's SEC was singled out as being uniquely captured, and in June, Warren called into question the very legitimacy of her .The senator pointed out how the SEC chair's personal ties to the finance industry have seen her frequently sitting out of enforcement rulings, as ethics rules dictate she must (White's husband, John, is an attorney for the securities law-practicing Manhattan-based firm, Cravath, Swaine & Moore).

"As you know, the impact of a recusal on the operations of the SEC can be quite damaging," Warren said. "If, for example, the SEC is split 2-2 on whether to pursue a prosecution, your recusal would mean that no prosecution could go forward."

Noting White's propensity to waive penalties to large banks, Warren then questioned what she was even doing in Washington. "You have now been SEC Chair for over two years, and to date, your leadership of the Commission has been extremely disappointing," the senator wrote.[141]

The White House wasn't at all concerned about this apparent *laissez-faire* stroke seizing one of its key regulatory organs. Josh Earnest shrugged off the broadside, telling reporters at a press briefing that "the President does continue to believe that [White] is the right person for the job."[142] It was after the same inquiry from Warren wondering why White seemingly lied about the timing of the CEO-median pay ratio rule.

* * *

The White House's defense of its SEC Chair followed something of a pattern—one which started with Warren launching into pointed, substantive criticism of the administration. To which, it would reply: meh (see, also, Chapter Six).

Amid her and Cummings' investigation of the swaps push-out, for example, Warren questioned if a Fed official—Alan Greenspan acolyte and top Fed lawyer Scott Alvarez—enabled Wall Street lobbyists to kill the bailout prohibition.

"Mr. Alvarez openly criticized the swaps push-out rule, saying 'you can tell it was written at 2:30 in the morning and so it needs to be, I think, revisited just to make sense of it,'" Warren said in February, grilling Janet Yellen about the extent to which the statement reflected Fed policy. "Did Mr. Alvarez provide input into the Fed's decision to delay the effective date of the push-out rule?" Warren asked.

The Central Banker admitted that she didn't know if Alvarez's personal disdain for the rule bought Wall Street time.[143] She did, however, after the hearing say that she "depend[s], with confidence, on Scott Alvarez' expert advice and counsel" and called him "a dedicated public servant who is committed to thoughtful public policy.[144]

And later, after releasing the findings of the "swaps push-out" repeal investigation, Warren and Cummings reported that the CFTC and the Fed couldn't (or wouldn't) give them a topline estimate of how many trades remained hinged on taxpayer-guaranteed savings (the $10 trillion number came from the FDIC[xii] and the OCC[xiii]). And none of the four regulators they reached out to did an impact assessment of the neo-liberal Cromnibus policy rider, either.

The inaction led Warren and Cummings to question "whether federal policymakers are sufficiently attentive to the risk" posed by public backing

---

[xii] Federal Deposit Insurance Corporation

[xiii] Office of the Comptroller of the Currency

for Wall Street gamblers.[145]

If not, then at least, per Michael Piwowar's take, left wing intellectuals should be easily able to rouse newly dispossessed workers from their tent cities—by citing data on income inequality that is revolutionary in its accuracy.

9. One Step Forward, Two Hops Back

James Clapper is not the kind of guy you'd expect to win a community center truth-telling contest. After Edward Snowden blew the whistle on covert surveillance programs in the summer of 2013, it was revealed that the Director of National Intelligence had flat out lied to Congress a few months earlier, when he told Sen. Ron Wyden in March that the intelligence community was not "collecting information on millions of Americans." Snowden later said the fib was something that motivated him to splash state secrets all over the headlines.

During a Senate Armed Services Committee hearing in **SEPTEMBER**, however, Clapper raised eyebrows with a stroke of brutal honesty and, in the process, set Chairman John McCain (R-Ariz) flying into one of his trademark rages. Months earlier, in June, Office of Personnel Management (OPM) servers were breached, reportedly by Chinese hackers. The White House saw sensitive information on about 18 million government employees compromised (data included Social Security numbers), and Congress was in a tizzy over how to respond. Clapper then suggested to the McCain's committee that, perhaps, it should say nothing. "People who live in a glass house shouldn't throw rocks," he stated.[146]

Clapper's words hung over the room for a few moments. McCain then jammed his finger forward to activate his microphone and sounded off. "So it's okay for them to steal our secrets because we live in a glass house?" he asked with an incredulous snicker. "That is astounding."

Clapper shot back: "I didn't say it's a good thing. I'm just saying both nations engage in this."

Although it is difficult to imagine such an exchange taking place before Snowden's disclosures, Clapper's frank-but-vague assessment didn't smack of a newfound desire to be transparent as much as it did a desire to boast—something McCain evidently had failed to pick up on. It showed, in a single soundbite, how Snowden's exposure of the national security state may have altered its public face, but the majority of its excesses—like its embrace of offensive cyberwarfare—would continue unchallenged in Washington.

* * *

Through its obsession with perception management, the administration seemed particularly keen on effectively preserving the permanent post-9/11 state of emergency—that is, if Orwell's famous maxim on history is correct.

Outgoing Attorney General Eric Holder, for example, had been widely lambasted by the press for thoroughly-documented illiberal attitudes toward freedom of information. But he saw things differently and really wanted Americans to make sure they got his side of the story. During a farewell speech in February, Holder claimed that the department has actually been quite lenient on whistleblowers and journalists, despite charging more conscientious leakers under the World War I-era Espionage Act than all other administrations combined (the law doesn't allow for whistleblower defenses).

"We have tried to be appropriately sensitive in bringing those cases that warranted prosecution," Holder claimed. "We have turned away, I mean, turned away substantially greater number of cases that were presented to us where prosecution was sought."[147]

The New York Times' James Risen, however, disagreed. An intrepid Pulitzer Prize-winning muckraker best known for unearthing parts of the warrantless wiretapping story a decade ago, Risen had been put under enormous pressure by the Justice Department to publicly out an alleged source. Former CIA agent Jeffrey Sterling had been accused of passing classified info to Risen about hamfisted covert operations against Iranian nuclear facilities. In the probe that led to Sterling's indictment, Risen fought off federal prosecutors' subpoenas for seven years. In January, he was finally forced to take the stand, but refused to answer questions. Federal prosecutors did not end up calling Risen as a witness in the trial

(Sterling was found guilty and sentenced in May 2015 to forty-two months behind bars).

Risen, therefore, could not hide his displeasure when he logged on to Twitter and found our story on the Attorney General's commentary. "Given Holder's speech today, I repeat: The Obama Administration is the greatest enemy of press freedom in a generation," Risen said, before following up with similar sub-140 character missives.

In one, he said that "Holder has sent a message to dictators around the world that it is okay to crack down on the press and jail journalists." In another, he pledged to "spend the rest of my life fighting to undo damage done to press freedom in the United States by Barack Obama and Eric Holder."[148]

* * *

It would be quite the fight, especially if transparency and freedom of information are considered part of the equation. The administration systematically prevented the American people from learning about the activities of their government. In some ways, its efforts last year were unprecedented.

The Justice Department, for example, put the screws on those tasked with conducting the most dogged internal oversight of the executive branch: Inspectors General (IGs). Although, by law, the watchdogs are supposed to be granted unfettered access to Executive Branch records, Justice Department IG Michael Horowitz repeatedly told Congress that his investigators were being denied info on whistleblower retaliation cases and federal surveillance programs. He noted the stonewalling started, in earnest, in 2010.[149]

But the shaming had no impact; the department doubled-down on its evasiveness. In July, its influential Office of Legal Counsel authored a memo granting the Attorney General justification to deny Horowitz access to what he had been seeking.

The decree had a ripple effect outside of the Department. Homeland Security IG John Roth slammed the legal opinion as chilling "vigorous and independent oversight."[150] Horowitz agreed with this in August Congressional testimony, before the Senate Judiciary Committee.[151] But if the administration's response to the committee is indicative, President Obama had no time for the criticism—no one from the Justice Department bothered turning up alongside Horowitz to defend its take on the Inspector General Act of 1978.

"Members should be able to ask the Office of Legal Counsel about this and many other problems with its opinion," Committee Chair Chuck Grassley (R-Iowa) said in his opening remarks. "Unfortunately, the Department refused to provide a witness from OLC for today's hearing." He called the decision "astonishing."

Sen. John Cornyn (R-Texas) agreed, claiming that "this is maybe one of the most important hearings we've had in the United States Congress in a long, long time."

"The only means to address this serious threat to Inspector General independence is for Congress to promptly pass legislation," Cornyn said. As of publication, the federal government's more than seventy inspectors general are still waiting for that relief.[152]

Meanwhile, the Obama administration still occasionally touts itself as the Most Transparent Administration in History. Earnest made the claim in March, for example, after being pressed about the decision to exempt the White House Office of Administration from FOIA—a move that reversed an Executive Branch standard of openness that dated back to days of Jimmy Carter.[153]

* * *

It wasn't all doom and gloom. Civil libertarians' most significant legislative victory in the post-9/11 era came in 2015, to be sure. But even that was very limited and rather happenstance—and it flew in the face of some notable opposition.

A target of intense criticism since Snowden's disclosures, the bulk collection of Americans' phone records by the NSA had been cited by reformers as a surveillance program ripe for curtailing. The Foreign Intelligence Surveillance Court dragnet authorized under Section 215 of the Patriot Act had proven rather controversial, after journalists Glenn Greenwald, Laura Poitras, and Barton Gellman reported its broad scope. The mass collection of phone records belonging to "US persons" did not quite sit well with the American public, even in the post-9/11 era.

But the person President Obama chose to run the Department of Justice after Eric Holder didn't see it that way. During her January confirmation hearing, Loretta Lynch maintained that the program was "an important part of the techniques we have used in the war on terror." She also defended it as "constitutional and effective."[154]

The courts have disagreed with her on the latter point—notably in December 2013, when a federal judge in Washington declared Section 215 illegal and called the collection it authorized "almost Orwellian." And the administration and NSA defenders in Congress have repeatedly failed to directly tie the telephone metadata program to successful counterterrorist operations.

But by Lynch's April confirmation, as luck would have it, the administration's undying love for the telephony dragnet was less relevant. Section 215 of the Patriot Act was set to expire on June 1.

In a legislative era characterized by inaction and incompetence (see Chapter Ten), even those who had no problems with NSA snooping backed slight changes to the law—a bill that would once again task telecoms giants with retaining call records covered by Section 215, forcing the US government to get targeted warrants before trolling Americans' call records. They wanted to reform mass surveillance in order to save it. Three weeks before the June deadline, the so-called USA Freedom Act overwhelmingly passed the House in a 338-88 vote.

But just as reformers saw in the looming expiration an opportunity, so, too, did one of the NSA's biggest and most influential allies in the Senate. Majority Leader Mitch McConnell (R-Ky.) wasn't prepared to curtail the surveillance state even the slightest bit under his watch. He manufactured a crisis with the sunset looming, then pressured Senators into approving a clean PATRIOT Act extension at the eleventh hour. How could they not during a critical time for national security?

With a week before the expiration deadline, McConnell then brought up USA Freedom for debate and whipped Republican senators to defeat it. They did. But to McConnell's dismay, the clean PATRIOT Act extension he proposed was promptly defeated shortly afterward; as were a series of short-term extensions that the Senate Majority Leader tried to ram through, to buy himself time to save the phone records dragnet.[155]

The gambit failed. McConnell was left with egg all over his face. As a result, the NSA was forced to briefly shut down part of its domestic surveillance program. On June 2, with his tail between his legs, McConnell brought up USA Freedom for a second time. It passed in a 67-32 vote, and was promptly signed into law by President Obama.[156]

From the senate floor, after passage, Pat Leahy called the procedure "historic." A co-sponsor of USA Freedom, Leahy feted his bill as ushering in "the first major overhaul of government surveillance law in decades." Many reformers agreed, hailing it as an important first step.

Others decried the fact that it left the wider universe of NSA surveillance programs largely untouched.[157] Some critics concerned with continued infringements of civil liberties were among those who voted against the bill—including Reps. Alan Grayson (D-Florida) and Justin Amash (R-Mich.).

As Snowden also detailed, the US government collects huge swaths of data from the internet. Though many of the programs employed in the online dragnet (like PRISM) "target" foreigners, they "collect" sensitive information about "US persons" never accused of any wrongdoing. In 2012, Sen. Ron Wyden and now-former Sen. Mark Udall (D-Colo.) cryptically described these then-secret internet snooping capabilities as containing a "back-door search loophole"—one that allowed the NSA and its partners to effectively spy on Americans without a warrant.[158] It would continue to exist after USA Freedom was signed into law.

To add insult to injury, by the end of the year, the intelligence community's internet spying capabilities increased dramatically, through the passage of CISA (See Chapter Three). Any historical analysis of USA Freedom and surveillance reform is incomplete without recognizing this.

* * *

The public would also, in 2015, learn tidbits about relatively new toys law enforcement officials have acquired to tap into the telecoms networks that reveal so much about it. Cell-site simulation, for example, is an emerging police surveillance technique that uses a device called a "stingray" to mimic phone towers—to collect information from mobile phones below. It was initially developed by the CIA to hunt insurgents, but repackaged for domestic crime fighting; despite (or perhaps because of) the potential for it to be used for mass surveillance. In April, the New York Civil Liberties Union reported on the great lengths that the FBI has gone to in order to keep this technology under wraps.

Documents the NYCLU obtained under FOIA showed that the Bureau only agreed to let Erie County Sheriff's officers use stingrays under a gag-order. On Feds' minds, specifically, per the agreement, were the prying eyes of journalists and judges. Disclosure, they said, "could result in the FBI's inability to protect the public from terrorism and other criminal activity." The FBI even reserved the right to urge Erie County officials to drop any charges, if pursuing them in court risked revealing sensitive information about the stingray program. The NYCLU cache also confirmed that this sort of surveillance was going on without any meaningful direct oversight. Eerie County only sought one court order for the 47 stingray operations it conducted between 2010 and 2014.[159]

Inquiries launched by Senate Judiciary Committee Leaders—Sens. Grassley and Leahy—eventually forced the government to be more open about cell site simulation. By the end of 2015, both the Departments of Justice and Homeland Security would draft policy guidelines requiring federal officers to abide by warrant requirements and data retention rules.

Those reforms, however, did not address how local police use stingrays; an oversight that could have serious consequences, as one Republican lawmaker noted. In a speech criticizing the directives as lenient, Rep. Darrell Issa (R-Calif) referenced allegations that stingrays have "been used to track policeman's girlfriends or wives activities and so on." Leahy also noted that he had "serious questions" about loopholes that allow federal agencies to drop the warrant requirement in certain "exigent" and "exceptional" circumstances.[160]

But neither he nor Grassley could dwell for too long on cell site simulation in 2015. Prompted by press reports, the duo had prodded the Justice Department for details about a variety of spying gadgets being deployed against the American people. In January, *The Wall Street Journal* revealed the existence of a DEA automotive data collection program—one that captures a driver's location, direction and photograph (in order to combat multinational drug traffickers, the DEA keeps this information for up to three months). The same month, *USA Today* also reported that at least fifty law enforcement agencies, including the FBI, have used radar technology, without a warrant, to peer into people's homes.[161]

Toward the end of the month, Grassley and Leahy complained to the Attorney General, noting a trend. The US government was increasingly employing Silicon Valley-style "disruption" to upset checks and balances.

"This pattern of revelations raises questions about whether the Justice Department is doing enough to ensure that—prior to these technologies' first use —law enforcement officials address their privacy implications," the senators wrote to Eric Holder. If and when they get any kind of definitive answers to these queries, the two will likely have many more outstanding questions unaddressed.[162]

When Rep. Paul Ryan (R-Wis.) moved into his new office in **OCTOBER,** something didn't quite smell right. The Congressman, 2012 Republican Vice Presidential nominee, and outgoing House Ways and Means Committee chair was set to assume the most prestigious and powerful post of his still-promising career—Speaker of the United States House of Representatives. Yet no one, including the 46-year-old himself, seemed to actually want the job.

To follow in the footsteps of John Boehner was a political deathwish. Hardcore conservatives' jubilation at Boehner's resignation announcement summed up the appeal of the gig. The outgoing leader acknowledged this, when stepping down—with an imminent threat of another government shutdown; one that would require another knockdown-dragout budget debate to avoid.

"I thought: today is the day I'm going to do this ... as simple as that," Boehner told reporters in September. "I really don't want the institution hurt. I don't want my colleagues hurt. I don't want to put my colleagues through this."

Not even a lifelong Ayn Rand acolyte like Ryan, though, could be sure of being able to weather contemporary right-wing purity tests. His small government credentials had been called into disrepute in 2013, after he worked with Sen. Patty Murray (D-Wash.) to pass a short-term budget. Some conservative activists blasted right-wing lawmakers who ended up endorsing the former poster boy for Medicare privatization.

If that didn't linger on Ryan's mind, when grappling over whether to accept the promotion, Boehner's own stresses undoubtedly did, the second that Ryan entered his new office—where he was greeted with what remained from Boehner's pack-a-day habit.

"You know when you ever go to a hotel room or get a rental car that has been smoked in?" the fitness-obsessed Ryan said in November on "Meet the Press." He vowed to use an "ozone machine" to "detoxify the environment." If only there existed Suburban Dad hardware that could make the Republican Caucus governable.

* * *

Before they even settled on Ryan, Republicans had already fought nastily—and very publicly—over who should succeed Boehner. A key player in this fight was the House Freedom Caucus, a group of like-minded Republican lawmakers who banded together in January—in this wacky Tea Party era of ours—to demand that the GOP tack even further to the right.[163]

The legislative band was unhappy that the Republican brass was strongly backing for speaker Boehner's second banana, Majority Leader Kevin McCarthy (R-Calif.), and splintered to endorse its own fringe candidate, Rep. Daniel Webster (R-Fla.). Then, caucus member and veteran lawmaker Walter Jones (R-N.C.) questioned the wisdom of the move, in an outcry that electrified the country.[164]

"Some of the most difficult times have been when our Republican leaders or potential Republican leaders must step down because of skeletons in their closets," Jones said in an Oct. 8 letter to Republican Conference Chairman, Rep. Cathy McMorris Rodgers (R-Wash.) "We've seen it with former Speaker Newt Gingrich and Rep. Bob Livingston, who ran for Speaker in 1998." Both men resigned after news broke of their extramarital infidelities.

"Let's learn from the past and not go down that road again," Jones concluded. When asked shortly after, he confirmed that he had been referring to rumors about canoodling between McCarthy and Rep. Renee Ellmers (R-N.C.). Two days later, on the eve of the leadership vote, McCarthy abruptly withdrew his candidacy.

"If we are going to unite and be strong, we need a new face to help do that," he said. "I don't want making votes for Speaker a tough one." Both he and Ellmers denied the allegations.

They appeared, however, to deeply disturb influential figures on the right; including, as *The Huffington Post* reported, a Chicago based-donor and serial emailer of influential right-wing Congresspeople and journalists. Hours before McCarthy stepped aside, Steve Baer emailed the would-be Speaker and other Republican legislators (including Ellmers) with the subject line: "Kevin, why not resign like Bob Livingston?"

Though the timing was certainly suspicious, McCarthy definitely didn't generally make the best case for his Speakership when he offended the rank-and-file by accidentally affirming theories about the political nature of the House Select Committee on Benghazi.

"Everybody thought Hillary Clinton was unbeatable, right?" McCarthy asked on Sean Hannity. "But we put together a Benghazi special committee, a select committee. What are her numbers today? Her numbers are dropping."

By the end of the year, the panel, led by Rep. Trey Gowdy (R-S.C.), had spent more than 20 months investigating the events that led to the 2012 killing of US Ambassador to Libya Chris Stevens and three others. It had been convened for a longer period of time than each of the Congressional probes into Iran-Contra, Watergate, and the Kennedy assassination. It was ongoing as of publication, months into the new year.

Gowdy and others who have much invested in the integrity of what is effectively a multimillion dollar taxpayer-funded Fox News unit were not impressed. Democrats, naturally, pounced on the remarks to cast further doubt on an already suspect committee. Upon stepping down in the race, McCarthy conceded that the Hannity interview "wasn't helpful."

Either way, Boehner eventually found himself turning toward a reluctant Ryan. After some arm-twisting, he got the Eddie Munster-looking wonk from Janesville, Wis. to take the job. After receiving guarantees the right wouldn't be ignored like it had been during the Boehner years, the Freedom Caucus agreed to endorse Ryan. It was summarily denounced by talk radio hosts and conservative activists as having stabbed them in the back.[165]

* * *

The Tea Party folk had a reason to feel betrayed, in the end. With nothing to lose, John Boehner dished them a final "Fuck You" in the form of a sweeping budget agreement with the White House and Democratic leaders—one that would set government-funding at above-sequestration levels for two years and hike the debt ceiling through 2017. Boehner referred to his initiative as a "barn cleaning."[166]

The implications of both the proposal and Boehner's description were clear. Year after year, while Boehner presided over Congress, conservatives attempted to use what were once routine procedures— funding bills and debt limit increases—as cudgels to advance deeply ideological proposals. Prohibitions on federal funding for Planned Parenthood and the repeal of Obamacare were among some of the more prominent conservative initiatives that ground Washington to a halt (financial deregulaton didn't; see Chapter Seven). Most notably, opposition to healthcare reform brought about a two-week government shutdown in October 2013. And it was a "debt ceiling" crisis manufactured by the GOP that initially led to the Budget Control Act, and the widely-despised sequestration limits it contained. But days before he was to leave Washington, Boehner took away Republicans' proverbial dirty bomb. In its place, party powerbrokers lifted sequestratoin limits and gave the federal government enough money to operate until after the next Presidential election.

Tea Party Congressman Justin Amash took to Twitter to decry the agreement as having, metaphorically, taken place in smoke-filled rooms (Boehner was present, so it wouldn't be wild to assume that someone wanted to crack a window). "This is how govt functions in corrupt, undemocratic regimes," Amash said. "Not how govt should function under our Constitution."

Paul Ryan himself said the deal-making process "stinks," but ended up supporting it, knowing it would help him avoid the kind of grief that closely followed Boehner throughout his reign. When the measure was brought before the full House on Oct. 28, it passed 266-167, with nearly every single Democrat joining 79 Republicans to see it through. A few days later, the Senate passed the budget framework in a 64-35 vote.

A few months later, in December, Speaker Ryan would use that blueprint to pass a $1.1 trillion year-end spending resolution that once and for all did away with sequestration. Republicans objected to the price tag, but enough went along with the vote because Democrats had conceded to lift the 40-year-old ban on crude oil exports. It was reluctantly approved by lawmakers on both sides of the aisle..

Rep. Tim Huelskamp (R-Kan.), a House Freedom Caucus member, called it "just more of the same era of bad deals in Washington." Perhaps he saw the writing on the wall:_The era of far-right hostage-taking had ended, thanks to the last-minute work of a man whose legacy is forever tied to it.

* * *

Although the Boehner saga contained arguably the most significant developments on Capitol Hill in 2015, especially given the improbable flurry of legislative productivity that followed—its gritty details didn't make for our most popular stories about the Congress last year. Those that did, however, did tell not dissimilar tales of right-wing incompetence.

Our most viewed post, for example, was a January report on freshman Sen. Joni Ernst (R-Iowa). A review of government farm subsidy data revealed that, despite campaigning on a hardscrabble background and an iron will to cut pork—quite literally, by bragging about her hog castration skills—Ernst's own family had received more than its fair share of benefits from the United States Department of Agriculture. We discovered that between 1995 and 2009, Ernst's family—her dad, her uncle, and her grandfather—accepted more than $460,000 in farm subsidies.[167]

The story didn't actually cause much of a stir, at first. A few weeks later, however, she was picked to deliver the Republican Party's response to the State of the Union. When she used her speech to tell the country about her family's humble roots (Ernst said she had "only one good pair of shoes" and on "rainy school days, my mom would slip plastic bread bags over them to keep them dry"), *The Sentinel's* WordPress lit up.

Numerous outlets picked up the story, including Fox News and *The Los Angeles Times*. The latter ran a headline, "Sen. Joni Ernst learned to 'live with her means'—on the taxpayer's dime," which was somewhat unfair, because there was no record of Ernst herself taking any ag subsidies. Not that Sen. Bread Bags had the right to complain about the bending of truth.

The Sentinel's second most read story in 2015 was a report on some less-than-sterile comments made off-the-cuff by freshman Sen. Thom Tillis to an audience at a Washington think-tank, the Bipartisan Policy Center.

Tillis, speaking broadly against government regulations, suggested giving restaurants a way out of rules that require employees to wash their hands after using the toilet. "I don't have any problem with Starbucks if they choose to opt out of this policy as long as they post a sign that says 'We don't require our employees to wash their hands after leaving the restroom,'" he explained. "The market will take care of that."[168]

While the Senators' comments could be dismissed as trite, they reflected an approach to governing that Tillis and others on Capitol Hill genuinely believe in; one that is obsessively and recklessly deferential to Corporate America. "That's the sort of mentality that we need to have to reduce the regulatory burden on this country," he said, after calling for bathroom liberalization. "We're one of the most regulated nations in the history of the planet."

A day after our Feb. 2 report, *The Washington Post* picked up on the story, running with the headline "Senator says restaurant employees shouldn't be required to wash their hands." The next day, Bloomberg ran an article explaining the "real problem" with Tillis' stance toward handwashing—it "isn't that he thinks employees should be allowed to opt out of post-poop hand washings, but that he'd rather make things easier for businesses than safe for consumers." Even "The Daily Show" got in on the fun, dubbing Tillis "Sen. Dunghands Von Fecalfingers."

The story followed the senator for a few days, before he claimed to reporters that he had just been making joke. "I think anybody who was there or actually watched the video and saw the context that I was talking about knows what kind of hogwash it is," he said. "It sounds like they got hold of a blogger to get the story spun up." Actually, senator, there are two of us.

11. "Religious Tests to our Compassion"

If, as the ancient wisdom goes, crisis brings opportunity, the Mediterranean Refugee Crisis in 2015 gave the Republican Party an opportunity to showcase how unrelentingly inhumane it is. In **NOVEMBER**, after French and Belgian nationals of North African descent massacred 130 people in Paris, Congress, led by its right-wing, held hostage the status of 10,000 Syrian refugees—the paltry[169] cohort President Obama promised to start processing in 2016, in response to the summer exodus.

The fear that closely followed the attacks unlodged a torrent of hatred from the right that Republican leaders have, unconvincingly, attempted to portray as alien to the party. Some seized on the assaults to call for confessionalist parameters to the US refugee program. GOP Presidential contenders Ted Cruz and former Florida Gov. Jeb Bush said only Christians fleeing Syria should be granted asylum. On the state level, twenty-six governors (including one Democrat, Maggie Hassan of New Hampshire) asked the President to freeze the Syrian refugee program entirely. Several vowed to refuse the refugees altogether (despite the Supreme Court ruling in 2012 that state-level immigration restrictions were unconstitutional).[xiv]

More threatening to the 10,000 would-be asylees waiting in the wings were proposals in Congress pushed by those who wanted to get more out of the dispute than a primetime interview. A bill that required Syrian refugees to FBI, DHS, and DNI background checks—a measure that would effectively grind admittances to a halt—passed the House five days after the Paris attacks, in a 289-137 vote.

The American people were marginally in favor of this. While only 28 percent supported religious screening and eleven percent were for taking

---

[xiv] The federal government "has significant power to regulate immigration," Reagan-appointee Anthony Kennedy wrote for the majority in shooting down much of Arizona's "papers please" immigration law, SB1070.

in only Christians, 53 percent backed a freeze on refugee admissions from Syria.[170] But the White House, to its everlasting credit, stood firm amid the panic, threatening to veto the measure and any bill that "would unacceptably hamper our efforts to assist some of the most vulnerable people in the world." President Obama lashed out, in particular, about the calls to take in only Christians, remarking: "we don't have religious tests to our compassion."

And then, on Dec. 2, a Muslim-American and his Pakistani wife shot fourteen people to death in San Bernardino, Calif. Before investigators could even find a thread tying the pair to extremist ideology[xv], it was the GOP that found itself improbably on the back-foot, led astray by its erratic newfound thought-leader.

* * *

Donald Trump, the celebrity billionaire heir-turned-turned pseudo-fascist front-running GOP presidential candidate, responded to the shootings on Dec. 7 by promising, if elected, to temporarily ban Muslims, including US citizens from entering the United States. Disturbingly, his popularity among GOP primary voters didn't take a hit, as a result. Nonetheless, Republican leaders scrambled to distance themselves from the idea, perhaps aware of its limited appeal.

"I told our members this morning to always strive to live up to our highest ideals to uphold those principles in the constitution on which we swear every two years that we will defend," newly-minted House Speaker Paul Ryan said in a press briefing, the day after Trump's announcement. "What was proposed yesterday is not what this party stands for, and more importantly, it's not what this country stands for," the Speaker also noted. Jeb Bush and Marco Rubio (R-Fla.) echoed this resounding denunciation, with the former describing it as "unhinged," and the latter calling it

---

[xv] On Dec. 16, the *New York Times* reported Tashfeen Malik and Syed Rizwan Farook privately discussed fundamentalist interpretations of Islam online, per the FBI's preliminary investigation. A few days earlier, the paper had incorrectly reported this discourse occurred openly.

"offensive" and "outlandish."[171]

But with Bush having rolled out his own discriminatory refugee policy[172] and Paul Ryan only offering qualified criticism of Trump's blatantly xenophobic campaign, key Democrats viewed the outcry as disingenuous; a matter of style over substance. The GOP fear factory was accustomed to pumping out more PR-friendly hatred—the sort that made Lee Atwater and Frank Luntz rich and famous in Washington.[xvi]

"This sort of racism has been prevalent in Republican politics for decades," Harry Reid said, in response. "Trump's just saying out loud what other Republicans merely suggest."[173]

Reid also took pains to stress that Ryan and Senate Majority Leader Mitch McConnell "have said they will support Donald Trump if he's nominated." Perhaps Trump could have proposed something "this party stands for" by having consultants first work on it for weeks.

One of Reid's Republican colleagues, after all, was making statements on the same spectrum—well before the Paris attacks. In October, Sen. Jeff Sessions (R-Ala.) suggested the entire refugee crisis was a fabrication.

"It has also been reported that as many as three in four of those seeking entry into Europe are not refugees from Syria, but economic migrants, many from many different countries," he said while chairing a judiciary subcommittee hearing.

When asked by *The Sentinel* about the source for the claim, one of Sessions' press aides replied with two links: one to a *Daily Mail* article that was thoroughly panned by *The Guardian*, shortly after it was published; another to a *Wall Street Journal* article citing an unsourced claim made by the leader

---

xvi   It appeared that Sen. Chuck Grassley (R-Iowa) was approaching matters from this angle, when he blamed Islamophobic hate crimes on President Obama, while calling for the repetition of dog-whistle talking points. "I fear one of the reasons for the regrettable backlash against Muslims in this country is the public's frustration with the president's repeated failure to acknowledge the actual nature of the threat we face," he said on Dec. 9. "His reluctance to utter the words: 'radical Islamic terrorism.'"

of an Italian far-right party, Matteo Salvini.[174] At the time of Sessions' statement, UNHCR data showed that 520,957 people had crossed the Mediterranean that year in search of refuge in Europe. More than half had come from Syria; 14 percent had come from Afghanistan, and 31 percent had come from war-torn or volatile places—Eritirea, Iraq, Nigeria, Pakistan, Somalia and Sudan. In other words, they were far from being "economic migrants."

And after Trump called for a ban on Muslims, Sessions wasn't timid about embracing the idea—or at least not rejecting it outright. He was one of four GOPers on the Senate Judiciary Committee who refused to endorse a softball resolution calling on the US to never discriminate against possible entrants based on religion.

In a 25-minute-long speech, the Alabama senator said a ban on bans could benefit "strange and dangerous cults and criminal organizations." The author of the proposal, Pat Leahy, responded with a brief dismissal, remarking that Sessions' refusal to back off religious tests was "the bottom line."

"There are people who felt the same way at the time my grandparents emigrated from Italy to the United States–they wanted to limit people because they were Catholics," Leahy said. "I'm glad they were in the minority at that time, or I assume I wouldn't be here." Sessions was joined in opposition by Sens. Ted Cruz, Thom Tillis, and David Vitter (R-La.).

* * *

Though many Republicans were repulsed by the idea of living among additional huddled masses yearning to breathe free, some managed to muster enough concern for their plight to call for more US military intervention—at least as far as Syria was concerned. They made numerous appeals to the Pentagon to establish a no-fly zone and a "humanitarian corridor," as images of Syrians risking it all to flee the carnage were beamed across the world.

"What you're telling us is that everything's fine, as we see hundreds of thousands of refugees leave and flood Europe as we're seeing now," John McCain (R-Ariz.) groused before to Gen. Lloyd Austin, at an October Senate Armed Services Committee hearing.[175] In November, Sen. Lindsey Graham (R-S.C.) said "the best thing we could do for Syrian people is to create a safe haven within Syria, a no-fly zone."[176]

In this endeavor, the GOP was joined by some from across the aisle, like Sens. Dick Durbin (D-Ill.) and Tim Kaine (D-Va.). "The absence of the humanitarian zone is going to go down as one of the big mistakes that we've made, equivalent to the decision not to engage in humanitarian activity in Rwanda in the 1990s," Kaine said late in December.[177]

At least the senators were, if nothing else, somewhat consistent. In April, before the extent of the exodus in 2015 became apparent, McCain, Graham, Kaine and Durbin had called for the US to create in Syria "one or more safe zones, 'with necessary enforceable mechanisms.'"

"These important steps would help alleviate some of the terrible human suffering occurring in Syria," they said in a letter to the President.

In September, the appeals were lent some currency by Gen. David Petraeus (Ret.)—the venerated former CIA Director and Commander of Wars, and the slightly-less venerated mishandler of classified information and co-founder of Iraqi Shia death squads. Petraeus urged the administration to ratchet up confrontation with the Assad Government, claiming "we have the capability to do a great deal, and, I think, we know how to do it capably and without undue risk."

"The fact is, we're already in Syrian airspace," he said. "We're flying over it all the time. We've already put boots on the ground in Syria—special mission unit boots." An aerial assault, he went on to claim, would stop barrel bombs. To complement the human rights-bearing payloads, Petraeus recommended the forging of "enclaves"—to beat back the exodus of Syrians fleeing the country.[178]

But just as the sabre-rattling were consistent, so, too, rejections of it by the slightly-less hawkish Obama administration. Throughout the year, Ash Carter told lawmakers that the American people weren't willing to pay the price.

"We would need to fight to create such a space and then fight to keep such a space, and that's why it's a difficult thing to contemplate," he told Durbin in May, nixing the corridor option.[179] In December, he went a step further, saying that "safe zones" could end up effectively worsening the refugee crisis, if they became "a place into which people were pushed, say from Turkey or Europe." The forced repatriation into a belligerent country was a scenario he characterized, mercifully, as "undesirable." [180]

And in October, Carter seemed to rebut Petraeus directly, shooting down his theory—that the US can scramble jets to fight Syrian aircraft "without undue risk."

"Were we to fly there, we would need to deal with the Syrian Integrated Air Defense system, which is a substantial undertaking of it's own," he said.

Carter also made a point to question the effectiveness of a well-executed no-fly zone. "Most of the civilian casualties inflicted by Assad's forces on the civilian population have been from artillery and obviously this wouldn't do anything about artillery," he noted.[181] It's as if humanitarian interventionism could draw the US into a wider war and its advocates don't care.

* * *

Some Democrats took the hint—that Americans neither would nor should commit to any kind of heavy intervention in Syria; particularly with a crumbling Iraq next door, as a tragic reminder of what can and does go wrong when the Pentagon goes all out. President Obama had first openly called for Assad's removal in late 2011, effectively declaring the start of US participation in a proxy war. The hundreds of thousands of people fleeing the violence and the proliferation of extremist groups inside of Syria and Iraq evinced its abject failure.

In late September, almost a quarter of the House Democratic Caucus called on the White House to engage with Assad's allies, Iran and Russia, to push for a political settlement. "Until we take this step, we will simply be managing chaos," said Rep. Jim Himes (D-Conn.).[182]

By late October, the administration seemed to agree, entering into a framework accord with Russia and other geopolitically important stakeholders. *The New York Times* said it "represented the first time all the major outside participants in a conflict now in its fifth year had agreed on the start of a political process to bring it to an end." By December, talks accelerated, and parties announced that in early 2016, discussions would involve Damascus and parts of the opposition.

Notably, the departure of Assad has not yet been agreed to, despite years of prodding on that front by American diplomats and their royal counterparts, from a number of Gulf states.

"There obviously remain sharp differences within the international community, especially about the future of President Assad," Kerry noted on Dec. 18. "But we've also seen in recent weeks – in Vienna, in Paris, and in other capitals, and then today here in New York–an unprecedented degree of unity on the need to negotiate this political transition to defeat Daesh, and then, indeed, to end the war."[183]

But if Republicans' inability to rein in their racist tendencies harms them in November 2016 (a likely scenario, given what we've seen thus far in the primaries), Democrats' own penchant to cling to vapid liberal militarism might see the war in Syria no closer to an end.

Days after the Paris Attacks, Hillary Clinton called on the US and its allies to carry out "more strikes," against the Islamic State in Syria and on a "broader target set." She also backed Petraeus—and contradicted Ash Carter's assessment—saying that a US-enforced No-Fly Zone would "stop

Assad from slaughtering civilians and opposition forces."

And during a question-and-answer period after her speech, Clinton said the move would "clear the air" of not just the Syrian Air Force, but of Russian fighters and bombers, too. She said it would strengthen our hand and yield "diplomatic concessions from Moscow and Damascus" in a hypothetical settlement; one that wouldn't at all be threatened by escalation, surely.

12. We Might Have Stopped The Fire

If, indeed, humanity is able to "slow the rise of the oceans and heal the planet," to quote a younger President Obama, the catalyzing moment may have come at the very end of the year. In **DECEMBER**, representatives from nearly 200 nations gathered in Paris under the auspices of the United Nations to agree on a plan to address climate change, requiring all signatories to submit proposals to cut carbon emissions over the next ten to fifteen years and beyond.

The odds that the deal will mitigate the worst effects of global warming are long. Climate researchers warn that global temperature must be held to below a two-degree-Celsius-increase over the next century to stave off the worst effects of global warming. If it goes to plan, the first round of carbon-cutting is expected to cool down the earth by half that amount.

If the accord holds over the next few decades, however, it might stop us from going over that two-degree cliff. Numbers aside, the climate pact sends a strong message to energy barons and financial conglomerates, at least according to its supporters. *The New York Times* cheerfully speculated that the accord could promote "a fundamental shift away from investment in coal, oil and gas as primary energy sources toward zero-carbon energy sources like wind, solar and nuclear power." President Obama said it "has the potential to unleash investment and innovation in clean energy at a scale we have never seen before."

All of that assumes, however, that the invisible hand agrees to shake on it. It also assumes that Republicans don't gain enough power in the intervening years to tear up the agreement. Senate Minority Leader Mitch McConnell promised to do as much when he heard the news from Paris.

"Before his international partners pop the champagne, they should remember that this is an unattainable deal based on a domestic energy plan that is likely illegal, that half the states have sued to halt, and that Congress has already voted to reject," McConnell said. As McConnell did in the

Tom Cotton letter to Iran that he cosigned (see Chapter Two), he threatened, on behalf of the next administration, to have the agreement "shredded."

It was a stark reminder, that for all the similarities between Democrats and Republicans—only the latter rejects widely-accepted science needed to enact planet-saving policies; and that the United States still remains one of the largest threats to the future of the planet, based on that fact alone.

* * *

President Obama, to his credit, seemed keenly aware of this and sought to accentuate the differences between his party and the GOP in the build up to the deal—perhaps worried that the accord's integrity could be at stake, if the United States seemed only half-committed (our reputation precedes us). Weeks before Paris, in November, his signature move came when he finally rejected the Keystone XL pipeline at the urging of his Secretary of State, John Kerry.

"Because ultimately," Obama said in a press conference, "if we're going to prevent large parts of this Earth from becoming not only inhospitable but uninhabitable in our lifetimes, we're going to have to keep some fossil fuels in the ground rather than burn them and release more dangerous pollution into the sky." He then boasted that the US is now a "global leader" in fighting climate change, and that "approving this project would have undercut that global leadership."

It was a momentous victory for the activists that had spent years agitating to stop the project. Citing the heavy environmental toll of extracting and refining the Alberta tar sands that KXL-boosters wanted to ferry to the Gulf of Mexico (and beyond), they had passionately and frequently demonstrated against the controversial vessel since 2009. Protests occasionally resulted in acts of civil disobedience and arrests in front of the White House

The president's rejection of Keystone also put an end—at least for now—

to a debate that mostly served to choke what remained of the air in Congress. McConnell spent his first month as Majority Leader working to pass legislation that would mandate the construction of Keystone—a bill that never had a shot of being signed into law, with the administration in the middle of its review process. After passing both houses, the bill was promptly vetoed by President Obama, who dismissed it as a sideshow.

"The Keystone Pipeline has occupied what I, frankly, consider an overinflated role in our political discourse," he said. "It became a symbol too often used as a campaign cudgel by both parties rather than a serious policy matter."

The President might have been throwing allies under the bus with the false equivalency (unless he was referring to pro-KXL Dems like former Mary Landrieu). After all, he had just vetoed an initiative rammed through a thoroughly right-wing Congress by a newly-elected Republican Senate. And when progressives counter-cudgeled, they tended to have "serious policy matters" in mind.

During a contentious Senate Energy and Natural Resources Committee markup of the KXL bill, for example, Bernie Sanders introduced an amendment that called on Congress to affirm four points: Climate change is real; it's caused by human activity; it has already caused devastating problems in the US and around the world, and the nation must move toward a renewable energy economy. The Committee swiftly killed the amendment in a 13-9 vote split almost evenly along party lines. A lone Democrat, Sen. Joe Manchin (D-W.Va) joined the majority.[184]

The Coal Country Dem told Sanders during the debate that he agreed with the first three clauses, but claimed it would "cripple ourselves" to unilaterally move off of carbon.

Perhaps befuddled that his colleague was openly recognizing a catastrophic problem while urging inaction, Sanders didn't budge. "Well, you got all four, Joe," he responded. The committee then refused to recognize what the vast majority of scientists deem necessary to avert catastrophic scenarios across the planet.

* * *

In other pleasantly surprising ways, the President upset the Republican Party by making notable efforts to protect the US from industrial contamination. Like in the late spring, when the EPA[xvii] finalized a rule clarifying that non-navigable waterways were protected under the Clean Water Act; or in January, when the administration shielded more than twelve million acres in Alaska's Arctic National Wildlife Refuge from oil exploration and extraction. Neither move earned the President Republicans' good graces. After the latter, Sen. Lisa Murkowski (R-Alaska) accused Obama as having "effectively declared war" on her state.[185]

But, as your correspondents have strained themselves to note, common themes that have persisted throughout the Obama presidency are secrecy and deference to industry. Both ran through the arena of environmental policy and public land management. In some cases, the administration's penchant for information concealment blurred the green image it was hoping to project.

In May, for example, the White House again approved oil exploration by Shell in the remote and dangerous Chuckchi Sea off the coast of Alaska. A previous survey by the oil giant in 2012 ended disastrously, when two of its rigs ran aground in extreme weather. The administration pulled Shell's permits. Then-Interior Secretary Ken Salazar said later, in an official report, that "Shell screwed up."

So when the administration gave the go-ahead for more exploration, critics, once again, rang alarm bells. Or they at least tried to. When a watchdog group called Public Employees for Environmental Responsibility (PEER) asked the Obama administration via FOIA to reveal on what grounds it justified the decision, the government refused to say. The Department of Interior told PEER in August that it wouldn't

---

[xvii] Environmental Protection Agency

produce any records until the drilling season ended, and that it would first allow Shell to redact trade secrets.[186]

"Frankly, this information should have been publicly posted already to give the public some reason for confidence after previous fiascos in this arena," PEER Executive Director Jeff Ruch said in a statement announcing a FOIA lawsuit; to force Interior to come clean before it was, again, too late. "After the BP debacle in the Gulf, this administration is again asking the public with a straight face for trust while denying them the ability to verify," he added in September, amid the legal battle.

Fortunately, it wouldn't matter. At least not in 2015. Later in September, Shell announced it was pulling out of the Chuckchi Sea, citing difficulty finding any oil. The administration, weeks later, canceled the company's offshore Arctic drilling leases. President Obama may have had the market to thank for greening his record in this case; especially with global oil prices having fallen by about $50/barrel in the twelve months before the reversal. Either way, the heightened possibility of another calamitous offshore-drilling disaster under his watch was averted.

* * *

But while that put an abrupt and anti-climactic end to one of PEER's transparency battles, another one continued throughout the year, with increasing relevance heading into 2016. The organization wanted to know what the government was doing to support those it orders to oversee protected areas.

Rank and file environmental regulators had increasingly become the object of antagonizing from right-wing extremists and militiamen opposed to the very concept of federal land management. In 2014, tensions peaked during an armed standoff at what is now commonly referred to as the Bundy Ranch, in Nevada.

Bureau of Land Management agents had moved to impound cattle belonging to Cliven Bundy, after it was found by a US District Judge that

Bundy had been taking them for decades to illegally graze on nearby public lands. Bundy and a team of gun-toting militiamen confronted the agents, leading to a week-long standoff. Eventually, the feds backed down, returned the cattle, and the Bundy militia declared victory.

After there was zero punitive response to the insurgency, PEER asked the Department of the Interior to detail what precautions it was taking to protect those it dispatched to deal with vigilantes. FOIA litigation, again, ensued, before PEER received a fraction of the information it sought. Among the cache disclosed by the Department of the Interior were internal emails sent during the standoff instructing Bureau of Land Management staff to "keep a low profile and not to wear anything that says you work for the BLM."[187]

The meek reply, and the lack of contingency plans for future had Jeff Ruch at it again. "Despite operating in what is self-described as 'the most transparent administration in history,' this exercise has been as productive as squeezing blood from a turnip," he said. "As it stands now – a year later – no lessons were learned, no precautions were taken, and BLM remains tucked tightly in a fetal position." He warned, prophetically, that the "perceived victory" by extremists at the Bundy Ranch is "likely to promote more violence" in the future.

It came in the first days of 2016, when sons of Cliven Bundy and other armed supporters seized the Malheur National Wildlife Refuge in Oregon; in protest, ostensibly, of both federal land ownership and federal prison sentences meted out to area ranchers convicted of arson. PEER was quick to say "I told you so," releasing a statement days after the occupation began, decrying "the lack of a coherent response to earlier confrontations with anti-government extremists."

After more than four weeks of occupation, the group's leaders, including the Bundy boys, were all arrested by federal and state troopers, during an operation away from the refuge. In the confrontation that preceded the arrest, police shot and killed one of the occupiers, LaVoy Finicum, after the militant allegedly reached for a gun. Within weeks, the rest of the militia members holed up at the refuge surrendered to police. Cliven Bundy himself was also nabbed, finally, by the feds, picked up in Oregon on his way to join the occupation at Malheur.

The US government, however, didn't have a similarly difficult time determining whether other types of demonstrators against natural resource management policy were possible enemies of the state.

According to a report published in May by the *Guardian* and Earth Island Journal, members of the anti-KXL group Tar Sands Blockade were targeted for surveillance by the FBI's Houston Office between November 2012 and June 2014. FBI records (released via FOIA) indicated that authorities had even cultivated an informant in the organization; a party to illegal activity to the extent that it organized non-violent civil disobedience.

The FBI later acknowledged it did not seek the necessary approval before spying on and infiltrating the peaceful demonstrators. That did not stop its agents, at the time, from reportedly promising to share with the would-be manufacturer of KXL, TransCanada, "any pertinent intelligence regarding threats" by the group against the company.[188]

No evidence of "extremist activity" was found—unless waging non-violence to denounce the imminent, irreparable destruction of the planet is considered "extreme."

Thanks again to our readers, members, friends and family for all their support.

AUTHORS

The District Sentinel News Co-op was launched in Washington in late 2014 to cover policy from a progressive perspective. It was co-founded and is currently staffed and managed by Sam Sacks and Sam Knight.

Sam Knight has been published in *Truthout, Washington Monthly, Salon,Mondoweiss, Alternet, In These Times, The Reykjavik Grapevine* and *The Nation.* In 2012, he worked as a producer for The Alyona Show on RT. He has written extensively about political movements and a push toward direct democracy that emerged in Iceland after the 2008 global financial collapse. He is currently working on a book about the subject.

Sam Sacks worked on the Hill as a Congressional staffer, and has worked in political journalism since 2008, as a writer, a reporter, and a television personality. He was formally a producer for The Big Picture with Thom Hartmann. He has been published in Hustler Magazine, which you may have seen, but don't want to admit.

NOTES

CHAPTER 1:

1   https://www.districtsentinel.com/state-spox-caught-criticizing-own-mubarak-line-in-hot-mic/

2   https://www.districtsentinel.com/king-fond-beheadings-honored-dod-essay-competition/ & https://www.whitehouse.gov/the-press-office/2015/01/22/statement-president-death-king-abdullah-bin-abdulaziz

3   http://www.state.gov/r/pa/prs/dpb/2015/09/247169.html & https://theintercept.com/2015/09/23/u-s-state-department-welcomes-news-close-ally-saudi-arabia-chosen-head-u-n-human-rights-council-panel/

4   https://www.districtsentinel.com/better-to-be-an-enemy-of-the-united-states-mccain-rages-at-limited-u-s-support-for-saudi-attack-on-yemen/

5   https://www.washingtonpost.com/world/national-security/saudi-arabias-king-salman-skipping-camp-david-summit/2015/05/10/2b6cad27-55df-47e1-a6c6-11a04020c788_story.html

6   https://www.districtsentinel.com/obama-admin-hails-alliance-with-gulf-monarchies-as-yemen-burns/

7   https://www.districtsentinel.com/obama-admin-hails-alliance-with-gulf-monarchies-as-yemen-burns/ & http://www.politico.com/story/2015/10/yemen-war-crimes-obama-215058

8   https://www.whitehouse.gov/the-press-office/2014/12/17/statement-president-cuba-policy-changes

9   https://www.districtsentinel.com/lawmaker-critics-of-cuba-detente-fail-honduras-litmus-test/

10   https://www.districtsentinel.com/lawmaker-critics-of-cuba-detente-fail-honduras-litmus-test/

11   https://www.hrw.org/world-report/2015/country-chapters/honduras

12   http://www.truth-out.org/news/item/32471-the-honduran-coup-s-ugly-aftermath

13   http://thehill.com/regulation/231117-bipartisan-bill-would-lift-cuba-travel-embargo

CHAPTER 2:

14   http://www.hughhewitt.com/senator-john-mccain-on-the-iran-deal-and-president-obama/

15   https://www.districtsentinel.com/in-iran-talks-obama-admin-considers-accusations-by-regime-change-linked-m-e-k/

16   https://www.districtsentinel.com/state-dept-rules-out-iran-secret-nuclear-facility-lavizan-3-allegations-pushed-by-congressmen-claims-appear-fabricated-by-m-e-k/

17   https://www.districtsentinel.com/state-dept-rules-out-iran-secret-nuclear-facility-lavizan-3-allegations-pushed-by-congressmen-claims-appear-fabricated-by-m-e-k/

18   Cotton Letter (placeholder link:
http://www.nytimes.com/interactive/2015/03/09/world/middleeast/document-the-letter-senate-republicans-addressed-to-the-leaders-of-iran.html?_r=0)

19   https://www.districtsentinel.com/gop-senators-attempt-to-subvert-iranian-nuke-deal-make-embarrassing-error/

20   https://www.districtsentinel.com/state-department-wont-rule-out-claim-that-47-gop-senators-broke-the-law/

21   http://www.vox.com/2015/3/9/8180933/zarif-cotton-letter

22   https://www.districtsentinel.com/war-profiteers-new-favorite-senator-pentagon-budget-should-approach-1-trillion/

23   https://www.districtsentinel.com/pelosi-near-tears-during-netanyahu-speech-calls-it-an-insult-to-the-intelligence-of-the-united-states/

24   http://www.haaretz.com/netanyahu-israel-s-arabs-are-the-real-demographic-threat-1.109045

25   https://www.districtsentinel.com/w-h-tells-netanyahu-words-matter-suggests-support-at-u-n-is-waning/

26   http://www.politico.com/story/2015/10/reid-obama-israel-palestinians-netanyahu-united-nations-214011#ixzz3uWwJOQKb

27   https://www.districtsentinel.com/u-s-confirms-it-stopped-arms-treaty-to-protect-middle-easts-only-nuclear-power/

28
        http://www.cruz.senate.gov/?p=press_release&id=2511&utm_medium=twitter&utm_source=twitterfeed

29   https://www.districtsentinel.com/obama-was-right-ayatollah-bans-further-talks-with-u-s-finds-common-cause-with-g-o-p/

30   https://www.districtsentinel.com/administration-says-nuclear-talks-wont-lead-to-iran-normalization-in-debate-over-french-word/

31   https://www.districtsentinel.com/kerry-diplomatic-malpractice-to-already-reject-wider-iranian-rapprochement/

32   http://www.mediaite.com/tv/obama-iranians-chanting-death-to-america-share-common-cause-with-gop/

33   https://www.districtsentinel.com/obama-was-right-ayatollah-bans-further-talks-with-u-s-finds-common-cause-with-g-o-p/

CHAPTER 3:

[34]   https://www.districtsentinel.com/fbi-director-continues-crusade-against-encryption-calls-on-congress-to-act/

[35]   https://www.districtsentinel.com/white-house-wont-dismiss-camerons-anti-encryption-crusade/

[36]   https://www.districtsentinel.com/nsa-joins-fbi-in-fight-against-total-encryption/

[37]   https://www.districtsentinel.com/loretta-lynch-joins-obama-administration-fearmongering-over-encryption/

[38]   https://www.districtsentinel.com/congress-still-skeptical-about-giving-law-enforcement-encryption-backdoor/

[39]   https://www.districtsentinel.com/comey-changes-gameplan-in-crusade-against-encryption-backs-off-legislative-ask/

[40]   https://www.washingtonpost.com/world/national-security/tech-trade-agencies-push-to-disavow-law-requiring-decryption-of-phones/2015/09/16/1fca5f72-5adf-11e5-b38e-06883aacba64_story.html?postshare=9031442410909976

[41]   https://www.districtsentinel.com/crypto-war-engaged-committee-leaders-pledge-to-take-up-anti-encryption-legislation/

[42]   https://www.districtsentinel.com/comey-lines-up-new-attack-on-encryption-urges-a-business-model-change/

[43]   https://www.districtsentinel.com/following-sony-hack-u-s-officials-re-engage-on-cispa-2/

[44]   https://www.districtsentinel.com/district-sentinel-radio-episode-4-dispatches-from-iceland-digital-discontent-in-america/

[45]   https://www.districtsentinel.com/leahy-decries-last-minute-attempt-to-pass-privacy-implicating-cyber-sharing-legislation/

[46]   https://www.districtsentinel.com/volley-of-proposals-designed-to-blunt-cisa-spooking-and-opacity-falls/

[47]   https://www.districtsentinel.com/along-with-net-neutrality-fcc-endorses-internet-public-option/

CHAPTER 4:

[48]   http://www.c-span.org/video/?325700-1/senator-bernie-sanders-ivt-news-conference

[49]   http://www.theatlantic.com/politics/archive/2015/01/democrats-facing-2016-debate-dilemma/457719/

[50]   https://www.districtsentinel.com/sanders-presidential-debate-plea-shrugged-off-by-pelosi/

51   https://www.districtsentinel.com/bernie-still-cant-get-respect-from-democratic-leadership/

52   https://www.districtsentinel.com/white-house-pleased-by-bernies-big-crowds/

53   https://www.districtsentinel.com/bernie-issues-minimum-wage-challenge-to-fellow-candidates-mostly-hillary/

54   https://www.districtsentinel.com/bernie-goes-to-liberty-university-to-enlist-economic-justice-warriors/

55   https://www.districtsentinel.com/bernie-sanders-nabs-endorsement-from-nurses-union/

56   https://www.districtsentinel.com/progressive-caucus-co-chair-endorses-bernie-sanders-for-president/

57   https://www.districtsentinel.com/second-congressional-progressive-leader-endorses-bernie/

58   http://elections.huffingtonpost.com/pollster/2016-new-hampshire-presidential-democratic-primary

59   https://www.districtsentinel.com/according-to-the-internet-bernie-can-claim-first-debate-victory/

60   https://www.districtsentinel.com/bernie-first-candidate-to-call-for-removing-marijuana-from-d-e-a-schedules/

61   http://elections.huffingtonpost.com/pollster/2016-national-democratic-primary

CHAPTER 5:

62   http://www.theguardian.com/us-news/2015/dec/31/the-counted-police-killings-2015-young-black-men

63   https://www.districtsentinel.com/obama-takes-bayonets-away-from-cops/

64   http://www.nytimes.com/2016/02/07/opinion/sunday/holding-sentencing-reform-hostage.html?_r=0

65   https://www.districtsentinel.com/in-lengthy-speech-blasting-new-york-times-for-criticism-key-senator-outlines-vision-of-criminal-justice-reform/

66   https://www.districtsentinel.com/top-gopers-dems-agree-baltimore-disturbances-highlight-systemic-abuses-cause-enough-for-revolutionary-spirit-in-america/

67   https://www.districtsentinel.com/grassley-gives-key-senate-booster-of-strict-mandatory-minimums-softens-stance/

68   https://www.districtsentinel.com/grassley-gives-key-senate-booster-of-strict-mandatory-minimums-softens-stance/

69   https://www.districtsentinel.com/post-ferguson-grassley-evolution-complete-judiciary-

chair-announces-biggest-criminal-justice-reform-in-a-generation/

[70]   https://www.districtsentinel.com/leniency-industrial-complex-strikes-back-house-panel-approves-criminal-justice-reform/

[71]   https://www.districtsentinel.com/white-house-refuses-to-comment-on-baltimore-surveillance-flights/

[72]   https://www.districtsentinel.com/fbi-running-surveillance-flights-around-the-country-rarely-seeking-court-orders/

[73]   https://www.districtsentinel.com/fbi-director-defends-baltimore-spy-flights-claims-its-helpful-to-know-where-are-people-gathering/

[74]   https://www.districtsentinel.com/feds-entrusted-with-securing-the-homeland-stalk-peaceful-protesters-twitter/

[75]   https://www.districtsentinel.com/obama-admin-knocked-by-congress-for-unwillingness-to-lighten-up-on-pot/

[76]
        http://www.slate.com/articles/news_and_politics/politics/2015/09/republican_presidential_candidates_are_blaming_crime_on_black_lives_matter.html

[77]   https://www.districtsentinel.com/more-evidence-ferguson-effect-is-pseudo-science-fear-of-crime-at-new-low/

[78]   http://thehill.com/homenews/administration/259419-white-house-rebuffs-dea-chief-on-ferguson-effect

[79]   https://www.whitehouse.gov/the-press-office/2015/11/06/press-briefing-press-secretary-josh-earnest-1162015

[80]   https://www.districtsentinel.com/dem-reps-call-for-justice-department-to-probe-sandra-bland-death/

[81]   http://www.nbcdfw.com/news/local/Sandra-Bland-Investigations-Nearly-Complete-Texas-Lawmaker-358958441.html

[82]
        http://www.theroot.com/articles/culture/2015/11/sandra_bland_s_sister_to_ag_loretta_lynch_take_action.html

[83]   https://www.districtsentinel.com/dem-reps-call-for-justice-department-to-probe-sandra-bland-death/

[84]   http://www.nytimes.com/2015/12/29/us/tamir-rice-police-shootiing-cleveland.html

CHAPTER 6:

[85]   https://www.whitehouse.gov/blog/2015/04/28/president-obama-why-transparency-matters-securing-most-progressive-trade-deal-histor

[86]   https://www.districtsentinel.com/tpp-finalized-gop-hates-tobacco-carve-out-special-

provisions-validate-dem-concerns-senator-claims/ &
http://www.huffingtonpost.com/2015/05/19/sherrod-brown-tpa_n_7338378.html &
http://www.huffingtonpost.com/2015/05/22/senate-passes-fast-track_n_7425614.html

[87]   https://www.districtsentinel.com/despite-requests-made-repeatedly-obama-wont-tell-sen-brown-if-t-p-p-is-a-giveaway-to-tobacco-companies/

[88]   https://www.districtsentinel.com/actually-the-t-p-p-would-screw-tobacco-companies-according-to-thom-tillis/

[89]   https://www.districtsentinel.com/tpp-finalized-gop-hates-tobacco-carve-out-special-provisions-validate-dem-concerns-senator-claims/

[90]   https://www.districtsentinel.com/actually-the-t-p-p-would-screw-tobacco-companies-according-to-thom-tillis/

[91]   http://thehill.com/policy/finance/249913-mcconnell-warns-obama-against-tobacco-carveout-in-trade-deal

[92]   http://www.npr.org/2015/10/08/446980193/orrin-hatch-on-tpp-despite-concerns-fast-track-authority-was-essential

[93]   http://democrats.waysandmeans.house.gov/blog/tpp-focus-investment-and-investor-state-dispute-settlement-%E2%80%93-need-reform

[94]   https://www.districtsentinel.com/tpp-finalized-gop-hates-tobacco-carve-out-special-provisions-validate-dem-concerns-senator-claims/

[95]   https://www.districtsentinel.com/tpp-finalized-gop-hates-tobacco-carve-out-special-provisions-validate-dem-concerns-senator-claims/

[96]   https://www.districtsentinel.com/lew-gives-insight-into-obama-trade-lobbying-as-white-house-prepares-to-push-t-p-p-behind-closed-doors/

[97]   https://www.districtsentinel.com/obama-admin-looking-weaken-regulators-banks-last-gasp-tpp-anti-localization-push/

[98]   https://www.districtsentinel.com/house-dems-accuse-top-obama-trade-negotiator-of-getting-high-and-spouting-bullshit-we-swear-its-true/

[99]   https://www.districtsentinel.com/white-house-granting-more-t-p-p-transparency-because-theyre-losing-votes-rep-grayson-says/

[100]   https://www.districtsentinel.com/i-got-your-fact-and-scrutiny-right-here-pal-sen-warren-issues-t-p-p-report-after-obama-accuses-her-of-lies/
[101]   http://www.warren.senate.gov/files/documents/BrokenPromises.pdf

[102]   https://www.districtsentinel.com/democratic-lawmaker-reacts-to-tpp-worse-than-we-thought/

[103]   https://ellison.house.gov/media-center/press-releases/rep-ellison-statement-on-trans-pacific-partnership-text

[104]   https://www.districtsentinel.com/obama-admin-boosts-t-p-p-membership-for-slave-labor-hotbed/

105   http://www.reuters.com/article/us-usa-humantrafficking-disputes-special-idUSKCN0Q821Y20150803

106   https://www.districtsentinel.com/senate-to-investigate-t-p-p-influence-on-heartless-state-human-trafficking-report/

107   https://www.districtsentinel.com/state-department-withholding-3-documents-from-senate-panel-corker-presses-subpoena-threat/

108   https://www.districtsentinel.com/tpp-malaysia-trafficking-report-inquiry-pivots-to-kerry/

109   http://www.c-span.org/video/?328262-1/state-department-trafficking-director-confirmation-hearing&start=2070 [36:30]

CHAPTER 7:

110   https://www.districtsentinel.com/u-s-boots-ground-extend-syrian-intervention-mission-creep/

111   https://www.districtsentinel.com/the-pentagons-syrian-recruitment-numbers-are-in-and-theyre-grim/

112   https://www.districtsentinel.com/military-chief-blames-failing-syria-strategy-on-ramadan/

113   http://www.theguardian.com/us-news/2015/sep/16/us-military-syrian-isis-fighters

114   https://www.districtsentinel.com/obama-seeking-approval-week-deploy-boots-ground-islamic-state-war/

115   https://www.districtsentinel.com/kerry-invokes-bin-laden-911-in-justifying-months-long-islamic-state-war/

116   https://www.districtsentinel.com/u-s-help-ypg-before-train-and-equip-general-reveals/

117   http://airwars.org/news/fresh-centcom-admissions-reveal-frequency-of-civilian-casualties/

118   https://www.districtsentinel.com/declassified-data-reveals-afghan-army-fighting-attrition-pentagon-dodging-accountability/

119   https://www.districtsentinel.com/blackwater-leads-failed-afghan-drug-war-reaps-hundreds-of-millions-of-dollars/

120   https://www.unodc.org/documents/crop-monitoring/Afghanistan/Afghan_Opium_survey_2013_web_small.pdf (p.40) & https://www.unodc.org/pdf/publications/afg_opium_survey_2002.pdf (p.33)

121   https://www.districtsentinel.com/u-s-splashed-43-million-in-afghanistan-on-a-500000-gas-station/

122   https://www.districtsentinel.com/pentagon-afghan-villas-sigar-report/

123   https://www.districtsentinel.com/sigar-hints-at-cover-up-at-now-defunct-pentagon-

business-liaison-program/

[124]   https://www.districtsentinel.com/msf-probes-kunduz-asks-if-u-s-thinks-hospital-was-fair-game/

[125]   https://www.districtsentinel.com/war-crime-evidence-us-leader-in-afghanistan-calls-m-s-f-attack-both-accident-intentional/

[126]   https://www.districtsentinel.com/u-s-special-forces-watched-m-s-f-hospital-before-army-bombing/

[127]   https://www.districtsentinel.com/us-military-now-preparing-for-decades-in-afghanistan/

CHAPTER 8:

[128]   https://www.districtsentinel.com/s-e-c-republican-pay-ratio-rule-saul-alinskyan/

[129]   https://www.districtsentinel.com/elizabeth-warren-accuses-s-e-c-chief-of-deliberately-giving-her-misinformation-in-private-meeting/

[130]   http://www.sec.gov/news/pressrelease/2015-160.html

[131]   http://www.c-span.org/video/?400558-2/us-senate-general-speeches&start=7809&transcriptQuery=swaps Senate Floor Speech. Nov. 10, 2015. 4:24 p.m.

[132]   https://www.districtsentinel.com/expanding-corporate-debt-one-of-several-threats-to-financial-stability/

[133]   https://www.districtsentinel.com/incomplete-loophole-ridden-dodd-frank-praised-by-white-house-for-stemming-china-crisis/

[134]   http://money.cnn.com/2015/08/26/investing/stocks-markets-2-trillion-erased/ & http://fortune.com/2015/08/24/stock-market-august-decline/

[135]   http://financialresearch.gov/financial-stability-reports/files/OFR_2015-Financial-Stability-Report_12-15-2015.pdf

[136]   http://financialresearch.gov/financial-stability-reports/files/OFR_2015-Financial-Stability-Report_12-15-2015.pdf

[137]   https://www.districtsentinel.com/highly-computerized-wall-street-set-to-face-new-cftc-rules/

[138]   http://www.cftc.gov/PressRoom/PressReleases/pr7283-15

[139]   https://www.districtsentinel.com/rapidly-growing-wall-street-managers-to-face-even-more-rule-proposals-sec-chair-says/

[140]   http://www.ft.com/intl/cms/s/0/4e9d566e-2999-11e5-8613-e7aedbb7bdb7.html#axzz3z3HNeRrl

[141]   https://www.districtsentinel.com/elizabeth-warren-accuses-s-e-c-chief-of-deliberately-giving-her-misinformation-in-private-meeting/

[142]   http://www.marketwatch.com/story/white-house-spokesman-defends-secs-white-after-harsh-warren-letter-2015-06-02

[143]   https://www.districtsentinel.com/elizabeth-warren-ups-feud-with-top-fed-lawyer-questions-if-he-helped-knife-dodd-frank/

[144]   http://www.americanbanker.com/news/law-regulation/warren-sharply-criticizes-fed-staff-over-dodd-frank-views-1072900-1.html

[145]   https://www.districtsentinel.com/cromnibus-put-taxpayers-on-wall-street-hook-for-9-7-trillion/

[146]   https://www.districtsentinel.com/spy-chief-hard-to-criticize-opm-hack-while-living-in-glass-houses/

CHAPTER 9:

[147]   https://www.districtsentinel.com/obama-administration-lenient-on-whistleblowers-and-leakers-holder-claims/

[148]   http://www.huffingtonpost.com/2015/02/18/james-risen-eric-holder-obama-free-press-white-house_n_6705078.html

[149]   https://www.districtsentinel.com/fbi-continues-thwart-surveillance-oversight-whistleblower-retaliation-investigations/

[150]   https://www.districtsentinel.com/inspectors-general-unite-against-security-state-secrecy/

[151]   https://www.districtsentinel.com/oversight-of-fbi-dragnet-surveillance-thwarted-by-department-of-justice/

[152]   https://www.districtsentinel.com/doj-lawyers-dodge-congress-after-controversial-memo/

[153]   http://www.usatoday.com/story/news/politics/2015/03/17/white-house-foia-rule-change/24900303/

[154]   https://www.districtsentinel.com/lynch-pledges-allegiance-security-state-headed-easy-confirmation/

[155]   https://www.districtsentinel.com/mcconnell-bid-for-clean-patriot-act-reauthorization-likely-derailed-by-rand-paul-filibuster/

[156]   https://www.districtsentinel.com/senate-passes-usa-freedom-act-embarrasses-mcconnell/

[157]   https://www.districtsentinel.com/blocked-amendments-to-usa-freedom-act-would-have-reined-in-more-abuses-disclosed-by-snowden/

[158]   https://www.washingtonpost.com/investigations/us-intelligence-mining-data-from-nine-us-internet-companies-in-broad-secret-program/2013/06/06/3a0c0da8-cebf-11e2-8845-d970ccb04497_story.html

[159]   https://www.districtsentinel.com/first-rule-about-stingray-f-b-i-club-dont-talk-about-stingray-f-b-i-club/

160   https://www.districtsentinel.com/lawmakers-highlight-weaknesses-in-new-federal-cell-phone-surveillance-guidelines/

161   https://www.districtsentinel.com/lawmakers-demand-explanation-fbi-new-radar-technology/

162   https://www.districtsentinel.com/doj-continues-stonewalling-senate-inquiries-on-surveillance-technology/

CHAPTER 10

163   https://www.districtsentinel.com/no-boon-anti-war-libertarian-progressive-alliance-freedom-caucus-appoints-reliable-militarist-leader/

164   https://www.districtsentinel.com/house-of-shards-mccarthy-resignation-throws-gop-into-disarray/

165   https://www.washingtonpost.com/politics/fuming-over-ryan-some-conservative-voices-turn-on-the-freedom-caucus/2015/10/25/8194f3ce-7999-11e5-a958-d889faf561dc_story.html

166   https://www.districtsentinel.com/budget-deal-struck-by-barn-cleaner-boehner-could-neuter-tea-party-until-2017/

167   https://www.districtsentinel.com/despite-campaigning-pork-cutting-family-living-within-means-sen-ernsts-kin-took-460000-farm-subsidies/

168   https://www.districtsentinel.com/freshman-gop-senator-im-okay-not-forcing-restaurant-workers-wash/

CHAPTER 11:

169   http://www.globalpost.com/article/6702267/2015/12/09/germany-million-migrato

170   http://www.bloomberg.com/politics/articles/2015-11-18/bloomberg-poll-most-americans-oppose-syrian-refugee-resettlement

171   https://www.districtsentinel.com/ryan-scambles-trump-fascism/

172   http://thinkprogress.org/immigration/2015/11/24/3725311/rubio-refugees-welcome-maybe/

173   https://www.districtsentinel.com/harry-reid-scalia-spouting/ & https://twitter.com/cspan/status/674264913863311360

174   https://www.districtsentinel.com/alabama-senator-refugee-truther-sessions-says-up-to-75-percent-of-asylum-seekers-in-europe-are-economic-migrants/

175   https://www.districtsentinel.com/u-s-help-ypg-before-train-and-equip-general-reveals/

176   http://cnnpressroom.blogs.cnn.com/2015/11/15/graham-theres-a-911-coming-and-its-coming-from-syria-if-we-dont-disrupt-their-operations-inside-of-syria/

177   https://www.washingtonpost.com/opinions/on-syria-us-military-leaders-offer-only-

timidity/2015/12/09/f1dd2b9e-9eb8-11e5-8728-1af6af208198_story.html

[178]   https://www.districtsentinel.com/petraeus-u-s-can-bomb-syrian-government-without-undue-risk/

[179]   https://www.districtsentinel.com/defense-secretary-warns-liberal-interventionist-senator-about-syria-plan/

[180]   https://www.districtsentinel.com/syria-safe-zone-carter-refugee-expulsion/

[181]   https://www.districtsentinel.com/pentagon-still-wont-call-for-syria-no-fly-zone-after-increased-russian-aid-to-assad/

[182]   https://www.districtsentinel.com/one-in-four-house-dems-call-on-obama-to-talk-syria-peace-deal-with-iran-russia/

[183]   http://www.nytimes.com/2015/12/23/world/middleeast/syria-peace-talks.html & http://www.nytimes.com/2015/10/31/world/middleeast/agreement-reached-to-restart-syria-peace-talks-and-seek-cease-fire.html?_r=0

CHAPTER 12:

[184]   https://www.districtsentinel.com/in-passing-keystone-xl-senate-committee-literally-votes-down-science/

[185]   https://www.districtsentinel.com/petrol-hawk-republicans-accuse-white-house-declaring-war-alaska/

[186]   https://www.districtsentinel.com/shells-trade-secrets-could-prevent-release-of-arctic-drilling-safety-data/

[187]   https://www.districtsentinel.com/documents-reveal-government-agency-quaking-under-threat-of-armed-militias/

[188]   https://www.districtsentinel.com/fbi-colluded-with-foreign-corporation-to-spy-on-americans-opposing-keystone-xl/

www.ingramcontent.com/pod-product-compliance
Lightning Source LLC
Chambersburg PA
CBHW022343290526
45786CB00014B/2378